Angelicals
REVIEWED

Also by Izak Botha

Blood Symbols

Angelicals
REVIEWED

IZAK BOTHA

South Africa
2017

Angelicals Reviewed

By Izak Botha

Cover Design by Fiona Jayde Media

ISBN: 978-0-620-75741-6

Contents

Religions build theories about the world and then prevent them from being tested. Religions provide nice, appealing, and comforting ideas, and cloak them in a mask of "truth, beauty, and goodness." The theories can then thrive despite being untrue, ugly, or cruel. In the end, there is no ultimate truth to be found and locked up forever, but there are truthful theories and better or worse predictions. I do defend the idea that science, at its best, is more truthful than religion.

Suzan Blackmore

Introduction

Many live their lives as if they have a soul. Yet, there is no evidence the soul exists. Neither is there consensus regarding the definition of soul. Customarily, the soul has been regarded as the spiritual counterpart of the human—a manifestation called spirituality. If so, the soul is a vehicle for human consciousness. But what if the soul is not breathed into man by God, as suggested in faiths?

Sadly, religions stagnate due to their precepts being frozen in time. Yet, their dogma thrives on untruth, ugliness, or cruelty behind the mask. There is no ultimate truth to be discovered and preserved forever, but there are sound theories and predictions that have proven reliable as they unfold. I, too, defend the idea that science, at its best, is more honest than religion. And although incomplete, hypotheses such as the big-bang and evolutionary theories remain compelling. The same should apply to the soul: despite scrutiny, the evidence supporting it must be credible.

For the greater part of history, evolution has gone unnoticed. After 13.8 billion light years of cosmic expansion and nearly 4 billion years of life on Earth, it is only over the past two centuries that the biological change of species over generations has found its way into our understanding. Knowledge of the process, however, does not mean everything is understood about evolution. As enlightened as we are as humans, we have yet to characterize *spiritual* evolution.

The purpose of this book is to posit that the soul has become part of human nature through eons of evolution. Rather than God bestowing a soul on man, life through evolution is achieving this feat by its own momentum. Spirituality is therefore a destiny, not a doctrine or belief.

Homo sapiens, until now, has personified the zenith of life. But is that the case? Allow me to show how *Homo sapiens* has been superseded by *Homo angelicansis*: the hybrid of two beings—the cross between physical and spiritual natures.

To discover how I reached this conclusion, read on . . .

Chapter 1

The Soul—Before Christ

The earliest evidence of the soul being regarded as the vehicle to immortality is found in the culture of ancient Egypt. For this civilization, the soul was ka, or breath. At death, a person's final breath represented the departing soul. For the Israelites two thousand years later, it was only after God had created man in His image that humans acquired a soul. *Genesis* records how, *"... the Lord God formed man of the dust of the ground, and breathed in his nostrils the breath of life; and man, became a living soul."*

Adam received a soul, and that soul was synonymous with an immaterial life-giving force. Although Adam was not the first human, the Torah and Old Testament pinpoint him as the first human to receive a soul when God breathed life into him. This text implies that God, in a singular act, created man. God *breathed* spirit into man and man became a living soul. From the text, however, it is not clear whether man was biologically alive before the breath, and even then, whether he was alive before becoming a living soul.

The interpretation of soul and spirit at that time is similar. In the original Hebrew text, soul is *nephesh*. Derived from *nâphash*, its meaning is to breathe or be breathed upon. *Nephesh* can represent a breathing creature, but in the abstract form it denotes vitality. Spirit is *rûwach*: to blow as in breath or to smell. It can also be *neshâmâh*, which is derived from *nâsham*: to blow away, a puff of wind or a vital breath, or divine inspiration, intellect, inspiration, soul, or spirit.

Describing the coming of the Messiah, Old Testament Ezekiel thinks even bones can be resurrected by spirit. The prophet's vision of the valley of the dry bones describes the Lord as a Being from whom emanates Spirit as the bestower of life. Dating around 600 BC, it is perhaps, for its time, the most insightful view of the issues of life and death. Ezekiel 37: 1 *"The hand of the Lord was upon me and carried me out in the Spirit* [rûwach] *of the Lord, and set me down in the midst of the valley which was full of bones, 2 and caused me to pass by them round about: and, behold, there were very many in the open valley; and, lo, they were very dry. 3 And he said unto me. Son of man, can these bones live? And I answered, O Lord God, thou knowest. 4 Again he said unto me. Prophesy upon these bones, and say unto them, O ye dry bones, hear the word of the Lord. 5 Thus saith the Lord God unto these bones; Behold, I will cause breath* [rûwach] *to enter into you, and ye shall live, 6 and I will lay sinews upon you, and will bring up flesh upon you, and cover you with skin, and put breath* [rûwach] *in you, and ye shall live; and ye shall know that I am the Lord. 7 So I prophesied as I was commanded: and as I prophesied, there was a noise, and behold a shaking, and the bones came together, bone to his bone. 8 And when I beheld, lo, the sinews and the flesh came up upon them, and the skin covered them above: but there was no breath* [rûwach] *in them. 9 Then said he unto me. Prophesy unto the wind, prophesy, son of man, and say to the wind. Thus, saith the Lord GOD; Come from the four winds, O breath* [rûwach]*, and breathe upon these slain, that they may live. 10 So I prophesied as he commanded me, and the breath* [rûwach]*came into them, and they lived, and stood up upon their feet, an exceeding great army. 11 Then he said unto me. Son of man, these bones are the whole house of Israel: behold, they say. Our bones are dried, and our hope is lost: humans are cut off for our parts. 12 Therefore prophesy and say unto them, thus saith the Lord God; Behold, O my people, I will open your graves, and cause you to come up out of your graves, and bring you into the land of Israel. 13 And ye shall know that I am the Lord, when I have opened your graves, O my people, and brought you up out of your graves, 14 and shall put my Spirit* [rûwach]*in you, and ye shall live, and I shall place you in your own land: then shall ye know that I the Lord have spoken it, and performed, saith the Lord."*

Giving life to bones requires breath, and therefore spirit (Spirit of the Lord). Yet, the soul is not mentioned. Either both the spirit and the soul are conceived as being the same, or else the soul is not seen as the life-giving force. As far as Ezekiel is concerned, it is not the soul that is breathed into a body to have biological life, but the spirit. The soul, then, must be something else. From this viewpoint, the soul does not give life, but like the biological organism, it seeks life.

The Greek writer Homer, credited with the ninth century epic poems *The Iliad* and *The Odyssey*, distinguishes between the soul and the body, but he is doubtful that the soul exists on its own. Once severed from the body, the soul is much like a shadow, and though the soul has the power to survive death, it cannot sustain life. The early writings do not include the non-material soul of later Greek and Christian thought, but rather equates soul with a faded, semi-material shade or ghost, whose life in the underworld is dull, destitute, and almost functionless.

Around 500 BC, in what is today Nepal, the teachings of Buddha emerged. Buddhism is unique in its teachings that the individual soul does not exist, but is an illusion produced by various psychological and physiological influences. Buddhism is the only religion without a God: a form of agnosticism, since it does not acknowledge or deny the existence of gods. For Buddhists, the constitution of humankind consists of five parts, known as *skandhas*—the material body, feelings, perceptions, karmic dispositions, and consciousness, which are all subject to continual change. None of the elements is permanent and therefore cannot be regarded as a blueprint for the soul, known in Buddhism as *atman*. It seems strange to deny the soul and yet have a name and rank for it. Buddhism teaches that belief in an individual and immortal soul leads to egoism and its resultant suffering. Buddha taught the doctrine of *anatman*—the denial of an immortal soul—and rejects the existence of *atman*; there is no belief in a concept of a soul or of a self that survives death. The Buddhist view of reincarnation is unclear and seen simply as a chain of consequences, but the subtlety seems lost in translation since adherents to Buddhist practice regard the dead as transmigrating souls.

The meaning of karma—the sum of the consequences of one's actions, both good or bad—is also contradictory. Karma is believed to be attached to the soul, especially regarding transmigration and reincarnation—the creation of each new body is then determined by the karma of previous lifetimes. The consequence of karma can be rebirth in a form other than human, such as animals, ghosts, denizens of hell, and, in fact, any form of life. Enlightenment is achieved through continual spiritual exercise and proper living, and only then can one shed the burden of karma and constant reincarnation. Enlightenment is only reached through a cycle of reincarnation through which individuals must pass to transcend human desire and suffering. Purification through reincarnation comes through opportunities to learn from the lessons of life.

If this is how enlightenment is achieved, then a record of each lifetime must be kept. One would imagine the soul to be the ideal vehicle for this information, yet the Buddhist has no belief in the soul. The paradox seems not to lie in the belief system itself, but rather that the philosophy is not consummated. The problem of an immortal soul in Buddhism persists and prevails in the doctrine to this day.

Philosophers from around 500 BC, and typically the scientists of the time as well, saw the soul as more than just mere breath. This prompted the idea that the soul is the prime motivator behind the mind—and perhaps even is the mind itself. Pythagoras, the sixth century Greek philosopher and mathematician, fused ancient mythology with the growing discipline of science. Known as Pythagoreanism, his philosophy combined ethics, supernature, and mathematics into a unified view of life, wherein the soul is a prisoner of the body.

Underpinning one of the earliest concepts of transmigration and reincarnation, Pythagoras believed the soul was released at death and— depending on the degree of virtue achieved—the soul moved on to a higher or lower form. In other words, the soul would undergo a series of rebirths in other bodies. The human, to purify the soul, was required to cultivate intellectual virtues, refrain from sensual pleasures, and practice religious rituals. Between death and rebirth, the soul would rest and undergo purification in the underworld. A series of rebirths would eventually enable the soul to become sufficiently purified to escape the cycle of life and death and to become eternally free.

Anaxagoras, the fifth century BC Greek philosopher, introduced the notion of *nous*, which is mind or reason. For him, the cause of beauty and order is the mind. Animals have a soul (the moving cause of things), but mind as intelligence appears not to exist in animals—and, indeed, not even in all humans. Although he distinguishes between the soul and the mind, in practice, Anaxagoras treats the two as a single entity.

Heraclitus, another fifth century BC philosopher, described the soul as cosmic ether or fire—the subtlest of the elements and a nourishing flame imparting heat, life, sense, and intelligence to all things, in several degrees and kinds. The spherical atoms of fire are identified with the soul, with both having similar qualities of universal permeation and the ability to set other atoms in motion by their own movement. His view implies that the soul is the informant of movement in humans.

At the turn of the fourth century BC, Greek philosopher Democritus expounded the atomic theory. Promulgated initially by his mentor, Democritus's view is that everything stems from minute, invisible, indestructible particles of pure matter (*atoma*), which constantly moved about in infinite empty space (*kenon* or *the void*). For him, therefore, atoms are the stuff of the soul.

Socrates, one of the greatest philosophers, connected the soul and the mind. Everyone has access to full knowledge of ultimate truth through the soul and only requires awakening to become sufficiently conscious to experience knowing. Plato describes the soul as the prisoner in the material body, with the body being the prison, tomb, or even the hell of the soul. His concept of the soul changes over time. In *The Timaeus*, he describes a world soul, created according to mathematical laws and musical harmony, which incorporates two elements: sameness (*tauton*) and otherness (*thateron*). In *The Republic*, his longest and most complex work, he describes three elements within the unity of the single soul: a rational soul situated in the head, a passionate soul in the breast, and an appetitive soul in the stomach.

The idea of a freestanding soul is the focal point of discussion throughout the history of philosophy. Sharing Pythagoras's belief, Plato considers the soul pre-existent, eternal, and entirely spiritual. Once it enters the body, it becomes contaminated by association with bodily passions, and congruent with the doctrine of karma, it retains knowledge of former existences. Both Pythagoras and Plato believed in the transmigration of souls from one species to another, or from one body to another, after death. Plato suspected the soul was released from the body after it had passed through a series of transmigrations. A soul of integrity, forged over several existences, would return to a state of pure being. A soul that had deteriorated during transmigrations ended in a place of eternal damnation.

Aristotle, Plato's most renowned student, was critical of the idea of the soul separating from the body and maintained that the soul is contained within the body as the form or actuality of the body itself. Nature is an organic system with different species, purposes, and modes of development. Humans have a rational soul that is higher than terrestrial species and only superseded by the higher order of nature—the heavenly bodies consisting of an imperishable substance, ether, which moves eternally through the cosmos.

Aristotle's definition of the soul as the first entelechy of a physical, organized body that potentially possesses life, or the forming principle of a body that has the potential to give life, emphasizes the union of the soul and the body. The challenge, though, is to determine how distinct the body is from soul. The soul of a living being is its capability to be a part of the activities that are characteristic of its own natural makeup: self-nourishment, growth, decay, movement, and, importantly, perception and intellect. Aristotle describes an organism with the ability to nourish itself, to grow, to move about on its own, to perceive, think, and be alive, and when death comes, to decay. The capacity of the organism to execute these activities constitutes its soul. The soul is the cause of the animate behavior of living organisms and is not separable from the body, for its very nature is capacity, not the organism. For Aristotle, the exception exists where the soul can separate from the body, and that is when it becomes pure thought that has rid itself of the trappings of personality.

Aristotle rejected transmigration or the reincarnation souls. The soul does not exist without a body, and though it is immaterial, it is not, in itself, a body. And although not a body, it belongs to a body and exists in a body of a specific kind. The soul is therefore spiritual substance encased in matter. He imagined a hierarchy of soul functions, such as the nutritive soul (plants), the sensitive soul (all animals), and the rational soul (human beings). The soul has little to do with personal identity and individuality, and he did not differentiate between individual human souls. This led him to believe there is only a singular soul, not souls. People only appear to have different souls, because they are different people. Despite slightly different bodies, all still have the same set of capabilities determined by the same soul.

Aristotle's view of the soul is the most comprehensive for its time. The competing views of his time appear limp by comparison. After Aristotle, though, Stoicism—a philosophy founded in ancient Greece and one of three leading movements contributing to the culture and civilization known as Hellenism—rekindled the earlier idea of *pneuma*, or breath, and despite its simplicity, greatly influenced the Empiric courts of Rome, and hence, Christianity.

In Stoicism, *pneuma* gives unity and identity to the individual. In lifeless objects, this unifying characteristic is state (*hexis*) and in plants, nature (*physis*). The latter are bodies and as such have causal usefulness. All reality is material, but matter is passive and distinguished from the life-giving or active principle, *logos*, which is both divine

11

reason and a finer kind of material entity—an all-pervading breath or fire. Living with nature and reason is living in harmony with the divine order of the universe. All existence is material, and the soul is breath pervading the body. The soul consists of the finest grained atoms in the universe, even finer than the wind and heat they resemble, hence the fluency of the soul's movements in thought and sensation. However, soul atoms themselves cannot function if not kept together by the body. If the body is destroyed, the atoms escape and life is dissolved. If the body is injured, part of the soul is lost, but enough is retained to maintain life. Ironically, the soul is the center of the cognitive and emotional life, its seat—the heart.

Stoicism, by advocating the brotherhood of humanity and the natural equality of all humans, equates with altruism. All people are manifestations of the one universal spirit, and all should live in brotherly love and help one another with good grace. External differences, such as rank and wealth, are of no importance in social relationships. Although preached, this part is obviously ignored by the Holy See—the government of the Holy Roman Catholic Church. Somewhat paradoxically, Stoics see all sins as equal, the sage as good, and everyone else as evil. The sage's actions resemble proper function with a distinct character of right action. Acting purely from right reason, the sage is distinguished by the ability to avoid passion. The average person has morally wrong impulses and passions, which are intellectual errors stemming from an inability to distinguish between good and bad. By contrast, the sage possesses wisdom, which is always right. Only sages are truly happy and free, capable of living in perfect harmony with the divine plan.

Chapter 2

The Soul—After Christ

The first century AD exposed one of the world's greatest intrigues when Saul, the Turk from Tarsus, persecuted Jews known as the Nazarenes but then later, nearly singlehandedly, founded Christianity based on the faith of the very people he had persecuted. Popular belief would have it that Christianity originated in Judea, the Jews were Christianized, and Saul persecuted Christians. This, however, is not true. From recorded history, Christianity had its foundation in Antioch, Turkey, where the interloper Saul (later Paul) appropriated the emergent Judeo-Nazarene faith led by Apostle Peter, proceeding then to convert Roman gentiles to a much-altered version of the faith.

Saul, by his own admission, persecuted Jesus. In *Acts of the Apostles*, he writes that Christ said to him: *"Saul, Saul, why are you persecuting me?"* He also persecuted the followers of Jesus, the Nazarenes, in Judea. Despite his life-changing experience en route to Damascus, in which he was struck blind for three days, Saul never announces a conversion to the Nazarene faith. Nevertheless, nearly a decade later, he coerces Antiochenes into accepting his version of the new religion. Saul had earlier attempted to preach to the Jews, but when they questioned his right and responded by stoning him, he turned instead to the gentiles. When Apostle Peter disapproved of his ministry, Saul summoned this rival for a debate. Known as *"the incident of Antioch,"* the outcome of this impasse is unknown. Clearly, however, Saul changed his name to Paul before continuing his ministry exclusively to the gentiles. The outcome is that Apostle Peter's trail grows cold, and apart from Vatican "holy traditions" proclaiming that Peter was crucified upside down in Rome, that Apostle is never seen or heard of again. Thus, amid considerable controversy, Saul, now Paul, established Christianity for the gentiles in Antioch.

With Paul as the founder of Christianity, one should at least take the time to see what the man says about the soul. Paul's letters to his churches describe the perfect human (*teleios*) as a tripartite being with body, soul, and spirit. Known in Catholic circles as trichotomy, this concept remains even today the official view of the Holy Roman Catholic Church. However, although the Holy See underwrites Paul's doctrine, it differs from Jesus's teachings, as recorded decades later in the *Gospel of Matthew*. There, the author of the first Gospel attributes the first great commandment per Jesus as "you shall love the Lord your God with all your *heart*, with all your *soul*, and with your entire *mind*." In this context, it appears that the *mind* is more of an attribute than the spirit. At no time does the Gospel equate the spirit with the mind.

Who to believe, then—Jesus or Paul?

For Paul, immortality of the soul and a place in heaven comes at a price. In *Romans 10: 8-10*, he suggests a twofold condition: oral *confession* that Jesus is God and *faith* that God raised Him from the dead. For salvation, believers must confess with the mouth and believe in the heart that these precepts are true. The content of the expected confession and belief, however, is astonishing. First, the convert is exhorted to believe that a human is God and then that this person was raised from the dead and now sits on the right hand of the Father. Yet, Paul, who wrote this, had apparently never met Jesus and was stoned by the very people who had.

Pauline doctrine is contrary to any established views of the time. Claiming that human nature is trichotomous, and not dualistic as promulgated by his peers, places him in opposition to great philosophers such as Plato, Aristotle, and Jesus. None of Paul's teachings are original. His interpretation equates with mythology dating as far back as the Sumerians. He then combines it with Greek and Greco-Roman thought from the preceding six centuries, and with hint of occult originating in the Orient, he regards the spirit as the highest and indestructible reincarnating component of the human constitution.

Paul's doctrine is illustrated in his letter to the Corinthians, where the soul merges with the body at the beginning of an individual's life, only to be superseded by the spirit at the end. *1 Corinthians 15: 42 So also is the resurrection of the dead. ... 44 it is sown a natural body; it is raised a spiritual body* [pneumatikos]. *There is a natural body, and there is a spiritual body. 45 And so it is written, the first man Adam, was made a living soul* [psuchē] *as the last Adam was made a quickening spirit* [pnĕuma]. *46*

Howbeit that was not first which is spiritual, but that which is natural; and afterward that which is spiritual. 47 The first man is of the earth, earthy: the second man is the Lord from heaven. 48 As is the earthy, such are they also that are earthy: and as is the heavenly, such are they also that are heavenly. 49 And as humans have borne the image of the earthy, humans shall also bear the image of the heavenly, so Now this I say, brethren, that flesh and blood cannot inherit the kingdom of God; neither doth corruption inherit incorruption. 51 Behold, I show you a mystery; We shall not all sleep, but humans shall all be changed, 52 in a moment, in the twinkling of an eye, at the last trump: for the trumpet shall sound, and the dead shall be raised incorruptible, and humans shall be changed.6 53 For this corruptible must put on incorruption, and this mortal must put on immortality. 54 So when this corruptible shall have put on incorruption, and this mortal shall have put on immortality, then shall be brought to pass the saying that is written, Death is swallowed up in victory. 55 O death, where is thy sting? Oh grave, where is thy victory? 56 The sting of death is sin; and the strength of sin is the law. 57 But thanks be to God, which giveth us the victory through our Lord Jesus Christ.

A study of the meaning of these words in the New Testament shows that psuchē, derives from *psuchō*, which means to breathe voluntarily but gently. It differs from *pněō*, meaning to breathe hard or blow, and *aēr*, which is to breathe unconsciously or to blow, referring to an inanimate breeze. *Psuchē*, by implication, suggests spirit. This is distinguished from *pněuma*, meaning *spirit*, or *rational or immortal soul*, and *zōē*, meaning life force or vitality, even of plants. *Pněuma* and *zōē* correspond, respectively, with the Hebrew *nephesh* and *rûwach* of the Old Testament.

Spirit, when mentioned in the New Testament, is nearly always *pnĕuma*, a current of air, like breath or breeze; by analogy, it can also mean a spirit (in a human), the rational soul, the vital principle, mental disposition, or even superhuman and angelic, a daemon or God.

Paul's intertwining of nature and supernature is staggering. In one swoop, he rehashes the supernaturalism of the myths, ritual, and magic of the preceding two thousand years. His use of *pneumatikos* re-introduces a supernatural element to spirituality. He also breaks from a dualistic interpretation, which excludes soul and spirit, yet introduces the mind. His reduction of the brain to a pumping believing heart and his rejection of the mind in favor of the spirit bears no logic. Despite its lack of credibility, Pauline doctrine was ratified by Emperor Constantine in the fourth century when the emperor established Christianity as the official religion of Rome. To this day, the dogma has been cast in stone as the unchallenged "Word of God."

Christianity has never successfully adopted the idea of transmigration. Initially, the Gnostics and the Manicheans believed in transmigration, but early Christians who adopted the doctrine were declared heretics by the Church. Yet, the resurrection and second coming of Christ corroborates this belief—transmigration and reincarnation, in and out of the spirit realm. The same reasoning applies to the second physical body, which saved souls are to receive on judgement day. These beliefs relate to reincarnation from one realm to another and to movement from one physical body to another.

The next principal architect of Western theology was Augustine of Hippo, who lived around the turn of the fourth century. His literary efforts, more than any other, shaped the Christian faith. Augustine, who formulated the doctrine of original sin, also brought a systematic method of philosophy to Christian theology. Human nature is in a state of sin due to Adam's disobedience, which renders humans powerless to change. As per his theology, believers are saved only by the gift of divine grace. Like Aristotle, he claims the soul to be the causal origin of the body. As God is the good of the soul, so the soul is the good of the body. Augustine also expounded the doctrine of emanation, in which God, as the *primeval* or *eternal one*, emanates the faculty mentioned above known as *nous*. From this intelligence springs the psyche or the mind, which is also the soul.

The sixth century saw the initiation of Islam. For Muslims, the pure monotheism of Allah (God) has been revealed through many prophets since time immemorial. Resembling much of Judaism and Christianity, Islam also teaches that God breathed the soul into the first humans, who are brought close to God at death, and that the coming judgment will see a resurrection of the dead, together with everlasting punishments and rewards. Angels and spirits are integral to Islam cosmology. Angels have roles, such as the transmission of God's revelation to the prophets, while spirits, known as *jinni*, inhabit our world, effecting influences on humanity. The angels neither eat nor drink and are free from sin. They are asexual and usually invisible, except to animals, although they occasionally appear in human form. The principal angel is Gabriel, the guardian and messenger of God's revelation to humankind. Michael is the protector of humankind, while Azrail, the angel of death, has the responsibility of receiving human's souls when they die. Israfel is the angel of the Resurrection.

All humans rise from the dead and surrender to the universal judgment. The Resurrection will extend to all creatures from humans to angels. After death, each human will be judged and will either receive salvation or be irrevocably condemned to eternal damnation.

Neo-Platonism, which sees the soul imprisoned in a material body, prevailed in Christian thought until the thirteenth century, when Thomas Aquinas accepted Aristotle's analysis of the soul and body as two conceptually discernible elements of a single substance. Arguably the most important figure in Catholic theology, Aquinas debates the soul at length and in lofty philosophical lyric. The rational soul has a sensitive and biological component or body and is the form (informant) of such a body. The soul is an incomplete substance, in that it must exist in the physical or vegetative body, completing the substantial unity of human nature. Although attached to the body, the soul is still seen as spiritual. It is not actually immersed in matter, and its higher operations are independent of the material or vegetative being. The rational soul is produced by special creation when the human is sufficiently advanced to receive it. In the first stage, when the embryo is developed, it has vegetative powers, after which a sensitive or sensory soul comes into being. Later still, this soul is replaced by a rational soul, immaterial and implied to arise as the result of a special creative act.

Descartes, the seventeenth century French philosopher, sought to explain how the soul-mind or immaterial directs matter to execute commands. If they two are separate, at which point do they connect and interact? In Cartesian dualism, he introduces the idea of the mind as part of, or perhaps intrinsically the same as, the soul. The trichotomy of the body, soul, and spirit is rejected in favor of a dualistic view of the body and mind. Accordingly, the mind and body must contain the soul. If the two components are separate, then it follows that the mental and physical models must be discrete. Although this soul-mind can direct matter, it is separate from the body it directs. Of the numerous theories posed by Cartesian dualism, none defines how the mind/body connection works. How does the mind know about the body, and can it influence the physical? And how does the body affect the mind?

In *"Cognito, ergo sum"* (I think, therefore I am), Descartes regards self-awareness as sufficient evidence for the mind to stand independent of the body. God created two substances that compose reality: the soul, a thinking, conscious substance located in the pineal gland, and the body, an extended substance with characteristics extending into a defined area of space. While extended substances act in accordance with the laws of physics, thinking substances act in accordance with the laws of thinking. The mind is not the brain; it exists without the need for spatial location and continues to exist after the death and destruction of our bodies. But what is it, then, that connects the mind and the brain? How can a non-physical mind cause a body to move? How can information about the external world make its way to our senses and cross the line that separates physical and mental, enabling perception from outside? Descartes's answer is that the states of mind causally interact with the states of brain. The aches and pains that cause us to moan and complain are the result of a brain state, which in turn triggers the physical reactions. Desires and intentions cause actions, which in turn give rise to brain states causing bodies to move, thus influencing the physical world. When the perception of physical senses takes place that involves causal transactions from the physical to the mental, this generates a two-way psycho-physical causal interaction. Taking place from the mental to the physical, it is an action; from the physical to the mental, a perception.

Cartesian dualism also assumes free will—a faculty akin to the soul. The supposition of free will is contentious among philosophers. Opposing factions see the mind as physical and a product of the brain, and they argue that since all subjectivity arises from outer world objective impulses, free will cannot exist. Scholars who found Descartes's ideas difficult to accept considered mind and matter incapable of affecting one another. Any interaction between the two is caused by God, who, on a physical change, produces a corresponding mental change, and vice versa. Others abandoned dualism in favor of monism, which maintains that ultimate reality comprises one substance; this, for most, is matter.

Two seventeenth century philosophers, Gottfried Leibniz and Nicolas de Malebranche, battled to resolve the difficulties left by Descartes's mental causation, abandoning the idea of free will and settling on the preservation of mind-body dualism. Both philosophers tried to separate dualism, characterizing humanity as both mental and physical, with the concession that the realms interact.

Malebranche, the formulator of occasionalism, denies that matter can interact with the mind, arguing that since knowledge is only possible through the interaction between the human and God, the mind and body cannot interact; it is God who makes it appear as if they do. Occasionalists identify force with the will of God. In its most extreme form, occasionalism promulgates that all mortals are devoid of fundamental worth and that God is the only true redemptive agent. Bodies cannot affect other bodies or minds, and minds have no causal effect in bodies of any kind, or even upon themselves. Only God is responsible for engendering phenomena, rendering both the mind and body causally ineffective. God is the one true cause.

Leibniz believed that God creates a blueprint that synchronizes a person's mind and body. His idea of pre-established harmony does not admit an inter-causal relation between the mind and body. Known as psychophysical parallelism, it teaches that God has a master plan, with the non-physical and physical running parallel to one another. Parallelism accepts that mental events correlate with physical and that mind and body exist in a pre-established harmony, ordered by God from the moment of creation.

Baruch Spinoza, another seventeenth century philosopher, taught that material and spiritual phenomena are attributes of the one underlying and infinite substance. The soul and body are a form of expression of divine essence. Since substance is self-sufficient and only God is self-sufficient, it follows that God is the only substance. In other words, God is all—the universal essence of everything that exists. As in Monism, ultimate reality consists of a single substance. To retain the notion of God as the one true cause, but without sacrificing the idea of cause and effect in the mental and physical domains, Spinoza abandoned Descartes's view of two components in favor of the double aspect theory, which sees the mental and physical as simply different aspects of one substance.

The quest to merge the soul with the mind, thereby establishing the soul as the informing agent, appears impossible. Association between the mind and matter, as far as philosophy is concerned, reaches a dead end. From now, physical reality is a component of mind. The role of the soul as an informant of the mind is rejected. Without verification of non-material phenomena interacting with a material body and causing it to respond through command, more knowledge of the nature of the soul-mind and body is needed. Without empirical knowledge, the discussion leads nowhere.

George Berkley, the early eighteenth century immaterialist, held that all material things are aggregates of mental ideas. He denies the existence of material substance without it first being perceived in the mind. A mind/body distinction cannot exist, because the body is merely a perception of the mind. The German philosopher, Immanuel Kant, believed the soul was only the subject of the processes of consciousness and not a separate entity, meaning that the brain is accustomed to classifying phenomena, which it later perceives as reality, but this reality is the outcome of its own activity.

In the end, neither Dualism nor Trichotomy proves the existence of the soul. Both fail to establish the soul: whether it exists, is separate from the body, or is the mind itself, which is the informant thereof. Millennia of intense philosophical and religious debate have failed to resolve the constitution and function of the soul.

The search for the soul continues.

Chapter 3

Occultism

Beginning around the seventeenth century, occultism rekindled the idea of the soul. Occultism, which is the study of the supernatural, is often misconstrued as Satanic practice. This is not true. Not everyone can make esoteric observations; hence, the mystery. Rather than being dark and evil, however, occultism merely explores that which is still hidden and unknown.

For occultists, humans have a triune nature consisting of a physical body, an eternal spirit, and a connecting soul. In the West, however, the soul is often confused with the spirit. Spirit in the *Oxford Dictionary* is the animating or life-giving principle in a person or animal and the intelligent non-physical part of a person. The *Cambridge Dictionary of Philosophy* records the soul as also called the spirit, an entity supposed to be present only in living things, corresponding to the Greek psyche and Latin *anima*. This, for occultism, is inaccurate.

Theosophy, the brainchild of Russian born Helena Petrovna Blavatsky, promulgates the idea of seven fundamental aspects to the human: physical, etheric, astral, ego/I, *manas*, *buddhi*, and *atman*. The seven bodies divide into a higher and lower ternary. The lower ternary comprises the first of the physical bodies, which are the physical, etheric, and astral, and the higher or spiritual ternary of *manas*, *buddhi*, and *atman*. Connecting the two ternaries in the center is the seat of the soul—the *ego*/I.

With the help of scripts such as the Sanskrit and Vedas, Blavatsky reintroduces spiritual knowledge to the West. In her *Isis Unveiled* and *The Secret Doctrine*, she likens the soul to a universal oversoul, an aspect of Brahman—the infinite, absolute, unknowable, and not open to speculation—and though the individual soul and oversoul are essentially the same, they vary in the degree of development. Spirit existed first and through a series of cycles was transferred to matter with the help of *monad*. After millions of years of evolution, with *monad* working its way into the lowest mineral body, Adam acquired a soul called *manas*. *Monad*, or the indestructible element present in every individual, finally expressed itself fully and consciously, and jointly with *manas*, became the conscious and reincarnating ego.

Building on the views of Blavatsky, Rudolf Steiner, the Austrian occultist and founder of the Anthroposophical Society, offers one of the most comprehensive views regarding spirituality and the soul. For Steiner, the physical component of human nature comprises a *physical* body constructed of solids, liquids, and gases, and the less dense *etheric* and *astral* bodies. The spiritual body consists of *manas*, *buddhi*, and *atman*. In the center sits the *ego*/I, illuminated by the soul. The *etheric body*, though a part of physical nature, is finer in vibration. As the life-giving force of the physical body, it suspends the physical nature in the condition called life. Without it, the physical body would disintegrate into the fundamental particles of atoms. The physical body returns to the mineral world at death, when the etheric body is no longer there to support it. Every organ of the physical body has an etheric replica in the less dense etheric realm and is visible to clairvoyants as a pale, luminescent vibration, extending about fifteen millimeters around the physical body and blue or violet-grey in color. Similarly, the *astral body* is the spiritual counterpart of the etheric double. Steiner characterizes it as the ghost, which people sometimes see shortly after a near-death experience. Finally, the *ego* or *I*, is the reincarnating *vehicle of consciousness*, which dwells within the sheaths of the physical aspects and is the unique element that distinguishes humans from any other living creatures.

For Steiner, there are three forms of soul: *sentient*, *intellectual*, and *spiritual*.

The *sentient soul* interacts with the physical senses. While perceiving an object, a mental image or picture is formed. On turning away, the sensory perception is removed, but since the memory is already formed, the image can be recalled. A process took place between the astral body and the ego, whereby the astral brought the external impression of the object to the observer's consciousness. For the awareness to last, the ego must receive it and make it its own. To be free of dependence on external objects, the human requires the *intellectual soul*. As the intellectual soul develops, the ego becomes conscious of external objects. Both the sentient and the intellectual souls work with sensory perception information and memories thereof. It is here that the ability to distinguish between external objects and the internal I is developed. Only humans have developed the characteristic of individuation. Finally, the *spiritual soul* enables the soul to become aware of its own nature and can become part of the Divine. The I is not God, but its essence can be likened to the Divine. The spiritual soul gives the *inner* knowledge and awareness and is distinct from the astral body giving the awareness of the world *outside*.

Steiner thinks humans have an even higher order of spirituality. For him, the upper ternary has a *Spirit Self, Life Spirit*, and *Spirit Man*.

The lower and most significant faculty is the spirit self. Through evolution, the ego forms an amalgamation with the astral body. Subjects work on themselves through the spirit self, which manifests in a higher maturity of our feelings and will. The second interaction is between the ego and the etheric body. Steiner calls this the *life spirit*. The work of the ego on the etheric body takes place irrespective of the individual's awareness. A person's life experiences become imprinted in the etheric body, transforming it into life-spirit. Although this is an unconscious process, awareness of it may arise through initiation and enlightenment. Finally, there is the *spirit man*. Known also as *atman*, it engages the ego with the physical body. Most people are unaware of this process and even those who are aware, are only dimly so. Complete enlightenment at this level is only reached with supreme spiritual knowledge and insight.

Steiner likens the soul of an unenlightened person to a pyramid. For this soul, the passions, desires, and emotions form the broader base of the pyramid. The apex represents the person's aptitude for superior spiritual consciousness. The opposite is true for the spiritually evolved soul. Represented by the inverted pyramid, the smaller apex at the bottom represents desires, emotions, and passions, while the broader base at the top is the higher degree of cosmic consciousness.

Occultism that suggests the soul rides on the back of another body is intriguing. The material body plays host to the soul for the duration of its life. The moment the physical part dies, the soul likely dies with it. There is no evidence that the soul survives the finality of death—yet. One might speculate, though, that one day the soul might achieve immortality.

Chapter 4

Mysticism

Before moving on to a scientific view of spirituality and the soul, it is perhaps prudent to investigate the murky waters of mysticism. Recent archaeological discoveries have revealed a period of cataclysmic floods that destroyed large parts of the Earth around 10 700 years ago. To understand what happened, researchers have reverted to the earliest recorded history of humankind, when the ancients—lacking the advantages of modern science—ascribed the origins of humanity to supernatural sources. These contain elements of magic and mysticism, but some researchers interpret the mythological accounts literally, claiming the ancients had recorded actual events.

Urbanization officially had its origins in the area between the Tigris and Euphrates rivers 7–8 000 years ago. Known then as Mesopotamia and spanning thousands of years, the land was inhabited by the early settlers, the Ubaidians, who developed language and writing, founded religion, and created political and legal systems. Their logographic writings, which date around 5 000 years ago, are the oldest texts ever found. Accounts of super floods predating the era and wiping out parts of civilization are recorded on a four-thousand-year-old tablet called the Babylonian Epic of Gilgamesh. Describing creation, these texts tell of inhabitants who provoked the censure of the gods, resulting in an earth-destroying flood. Just like Noah, the god king Zisudra built a vessel to survive the floods. Two gods, An and Enlil, were so grateful to Zisudra for building this Ark that they decided to make him immortal.

It is from the mores of humans achieving immortality that I continue my quest for the soul. The conception of immortality seems indicative of a change that had taken place in which humans perceived not only life and death, but themselves as well.

The notion of Adam preceding Noah is noteworthy, for it suggests humans with souls preceded the great floods. Adam, however, dates around 6 000 years ago, coming after the super floods of 11 700 years ago. Timewise, Adam does not match the archaeological finds of our day. Seen in reverse, the first awareness of the soul would also coincide with the awareness of the ka of the Egyptians, which dates around 5–6 000 years ago, well into the urbanization at Mesopotamia. Notwithstanding, archaeology's rewriting of history has led to unusual hypotheses of late. The reason for including these is the uneasy place it leaves the existence of the soul. Following, then, are accounts where contemporary researchers have come up with unusual ideas regarding our ancestral origins.

Atlantis and Lemuria

The classical Greek philosopher Plato, in *Timaeus* and *Critias*, writes of the lost civilization of Atlantis: an ancient island kingdom buried beneath the sea—a utopian commonwealth with a palace, waterways, docks, horse racing tracks, public baths, gardens, and temples filled with gold statues. Not much is said about Atlantis after Plato, but that changed when Ignatius Donnelly resurrected the acropolis in the nineteenth century, making it the birthplace of modern civilization.

Then there is the legend of the land of Lemuria or Mu, situated somewhere in the Pacific Ocean, which Polynesians hold as the motherland of all humankind. The Spanish priest Diego de Landa, who—after burning many original Mayan books—became an avid scholar of Mayan tradition, believed that the Mayan ancestors were the ten lost tribes of Israel. Diego intimidated the indigenous people into giving him false translations of their alphabet. Charles-Etienne Brasseur de Bourbourg then used it to translate the Troano Codex, and by stretching the credibility of the translation by attributing "Mu" to two symbols, he produced the grand tale of a lost continent.

Author and researcher Graham Hancock spent years cataloguing myths of a city with seven temples, submerged beneath the sea. Following up on Hancock's theories, the Dorset-based Scientific Exploration Society (SES) and marine archaeologists from India's National Institute of Oceanography found submerged temples near Mahabalipuram, in Tamil Nadu, South India. Off the Tranquebar-Poompuhur coast and submerged by 23 meters lie a U-shaped architectural structure, perhaps the remains of an unknown culture. Further along, in north-western India's Gulf of Kutch, the sea level 10 000 years ago was 60 meters lower than it is today, making it thousands of years older than any of the monuments found at ancient Mesopotamia and Egypt. South West of Japan's Ryukyu Islands, and at a depth of 30 meters, lies a structure believed to be 20 000 years old. Its ceremonial center, with promenades and pylons, measures 150 meters long, 50 wide and 20 high. This early Japanese civilization is concomitant with the age of Neolithic hunters and gatherers, so it is easy to see why these monuments present such an enigma.

The parallelism of reality and myth has led many to believe the pre-Mesopotamian civilizations resulted from extraterrestrial intervention. Some credit mysterious beings, such as gods, angels, and aliens from alternative dimensions, with creating our past. The idea of aliens initiating the advanced culture of pre-Mesopotamia calls for serious debate. All cultures feature myth to describe their origins. The idea of it representing actual history, though, requires investigation.

Giving myths a literal interpretation creates problems as far as the soul is concerned. If true and aliens created humanity, the question of spirituality and the soul becomes all important. It might sound silly, but if the gods—or aliens—sexually harassed Earthlings, we should take heed. Hypotheses of otherworldly creatures are threefold: *extraterrestrials* from other cosmic destinations, *soul beings* from the astral plane seeking earthly experience, and *hybrid beings* with supernatural powers comprising one and two. Let me explain.

Extraterrestrials

Belief in deities—gods from the heavens—originates in Mesopotamia. Codified on a set of pillars around 3 800 years ago, the first written laws for individuals and society describe how, during the reign of Marduk, the Babylonian god became a leader in the pantheon of deities known as the Anunnaki or Igigi. Records of similar deities appear in the Old Testament, where the Nephilim—also referred to as giants—roamed the Earth, while the "sons of God" came onto the daughters of men, impregnating them.

Originally, the Bible verse of sons of God was interpreted as sons of Yahweh. The idea of the offspring of the Creator God having intercourse with Earthlings gave rise to the less challenging precept of "sons of gods" being the Nephilim and Anunnaki. Combining the respective mythologies, however, contemporary writers now interpret sons of gods as extraterrestrials from alternative places in the universe. Thus, writers such as Erich von Daniken and Zechariah Sitchin suggest the gods and their sons came to Earth in spaceships, thereby explaining the sudden evolutionary quantum leap of 12 000 years ago.

Von Daniken is passionate about aliens and thinks the sons of god coming from the sky translates into extraterrestrial crossbreeding, resulting in humans receiving genetic messages inconsistent with their own. Already knowing they would find life on the blue planet, a giant mothership entered our solar system. After altering the DNA of some Earthlings and turning them into *Homo sapiens*, they left. Von Daniken suggests that biblical Eve was visited by a UFO. Eve looks towards heaven to see a chariot of lights pulled by four gleaming eagles of magnificent beauty. Von Daniken thinks Eve was first to witness a UFO and thinks that since the text mentions the Lord mounting the chariot, this must have been the Lord who created Adam and Eve. His views on sons of gods and renegade angels is that the seduction of Eve resulted in two races evolving from her offspring: Cain and Abel. With the collapse of morality and the sexual excesses in Sodom, fallen angels descended from the heavens and took human wives. Their giant offspring, the Nephilim or Anunnaki, kept busy by robbing, plundering, and spilling blood, and producing offspring—as many as six at a time. Ultimately, the crossbreeding with people produced creatures inconsistent with the planned *Homo sapiens*. This is the original sin of mythology. Humans inheriting the wrong genetic messages caused much grief to the Lord.

Von Daniken uses the *Book of Enoch*, a collection of works by first and second centuries BC authors and named after the Hebrew patriarch Enoch, to explain what happens when angels mutiny on Earth. In *Enoch 6:1-6*, the children of men multiplied, leaving a generation of daughters. The angels and sons of heaven lusted after them, telling themselves to take the Earthlings as wives and let them bear children. Their leader, Semiaza, asked them to restrain themselves, for he would be held responsible. However, the angels disobeyed him, taking wives and indulging in impure acts. Running out of food, the extraterrestrials turned against their wives, devouring them. All this occurred, while the good angels observed from above.

Russian born author Zechariah Sitchin puts forward the idea of a tenth planet, called Nibiru. After a clash between Nibiru and Mars, the inhabitants from the two planets came to live on Earth. Like Von Daniken, the main theme of Sitchin's work questions the sudden appearance of Sumer, seemingly out of nowhere. Excavated in Sumerian cities are texts and illustrations listing stars and constellations, as well as manuals observing the rising and setting of stars and planets. The planets orbiting the sun seem to be in their correct order; as are the stars and constellations in their heavenly locations. One text featuring a cataclysmic event even shows the distances between the planets. Also documented is a collision that resulted in the tenth planet from which the Anunnaki originated.

Sitchin thinks the Anunnaki came to Earth 450 000 years ago to mine gold in and around Zimbabwe. The elliptical orbit of Nibiru made a loop through our solar system, acting as a moving observatory from which investigations of our planets took place. The Anunnaki were facing ecological deterioration, making life on Nibiru increasingly difficult. After discovering gold on Earth, they missioned here to mine the precious metal. To increase their atmosphere, they would suspend particles of gold above their planet. Their initial attempt to get it from the Persian Gulf failed, so they started mining in south-eastern Africa. The gold was shipped home from bases in the Middle East, but around 300 000 years ago, some mutinied. With the Anunnaki initially doing their own mining, some rebelled, forcing the Anunnaki elite to create a slave race to do the work. The chief scientist and the chief medical officer used genetic manipulation and in-vitro fertilization, creating the first slave miners—*Homo sapiens*.

Alien Souls

To accompany the *ka*, or soul, into the next world, the Egyptians preserved the body of their deceased—hence, mummification and the pyramids. Evidence of settlements from 7 000 BC exists, but it was 4–5 000 years ago that the settlements along the Nile valley invented sophisticated irrigation and tombs. Among the rituals for the dead is a collection of funerary texts called the *Book of the Dead*, which contain magical formulae, hymns, and prayers that are believed to guide and protect the ka on its journey.

Burying the dead was of great import, and funerary rituals for the ancient Egyptians are of the most luxurious ever found. The departed—routinely called the *living*, the coffin the *chest of the living*, and the tomb the *lord of life*—was to revisit the Earthly tomb. The disembodied ka went to the heavenly realm, where grain grew twice the height of a man and life was a glorified version of that on Earth. The *ka* was dependent for its existence on the body, making preservation of the corpse crucial.

The idea of transmigration continued to evolve. Soon, the soul departed from the body, entering a new body at the next birth. The Egyptians later believed the soul could leave the body during sleep. Later still, the soul transmigrated to an infant of the dead person's family. This was a useful way of explaining family resemblance. For the Babylonians, the life of the king related to the life of the land, crops, herds, and its people. Unlike the Egyptian king, though, the Babylonian king was not divine but merely a representative of God. The underworld is in the *waters of life* and Marduk, who is *one who brings the dead to life*, extrapolates belief in resurrection. Hinduism in India, dating back to the third millennium BC, held that the body is inhabited by a single soul, which separates from the body at death and during sleep, passing in and out of the mouth or nostrils. While separated from the body after death, the soul seeks to inhabit a new body and if necessary enters that of lower forms of life, such as animals. For Hindus, reincarnation occurred when souls transmigrated to new members of the same family.

The ancient Greeks of 500 BC associated transmigration with the philosophy of Pythagoras who considered the soul immortal. After a series of rebirths—each following a period of purification in the underworld—the soul became free from the cycle of reincarnation. Delivery from the body occurred only after the soul had passed through a series of transmigrations. When the soul maintained good character, it returned to a state of pure being.

Judaism and Christianity have never adopted the idea of transmigration. Among Jews, only the mystical Cabbalists accepts the idea. The Gnostics and the Manicheans also believed in transmigration, but early Christians adopting Gnostic and Manichaean doctrines were declared heretics by the Church. Christianity's repudiation of reincarnation was linked to a belief in judgment after death. To strengthen the Church, the dogma of one life that merited eternal reward or damnation was promulgated. The concepts of transmigration and reincarnation did not change much until the late nineteenth century, when occultists added mystique to the already elusive ideas. With the Church losing its grip on cultic practices and freedom of speech allowing varying beliefs, practitioners shared their knowledge.

Occultism introduces the idea of root races: spiritual entities occupying embryos of human before birth. Strongly influenced by Hinduism and Buddhism, Blavatsky introduced the idea of the transmigration and reincarnation of souls from alternative realms to experience life in human bodies. She introduces the concept of humans not acquiring souls, but rather that souls, over millions of years, having taken on human form. Spirit beings originated from the etheric realm and from there worked their way up into the astral plane. Eventually, they entered the physical phase, which she thinks is the Lemuria epoch. Lemuria and Atlantis, for her, are the third and fourth epochs of the seven root races.

Called also the Adamic race, the first root race was as ethereal as ours is material. Possessing only the faculty of hearing, these beings dwelled in protean astral bodies. Evolving in northern Asia, the second root race refers to the Hyperboreans or Reptilians. The first and second root races were not physical, but spiritual. The third root race originated in Lemuria, emerging around eighteen million years ago and ending five million years ago. The inhabitants were not humans yet, but had learned to take on physical form. They were egg laying and possessed a third eye, which gave them psychic powers and allowed them to function without a brain. Originally sexless, the Lemuria race separated into male and female and developed womb birth. From here evolved the fourth root race of Atlantis. For Blavatsky, these Atlanteans were fully developed humans, sharing the basic characteristics of today's *Homo sapiens*. Humanity today represents the fifth root race or Aryan race. The sixth and seventh root races are still to come, and details about them are ill-defined.

Counselling psychologist and certified master hypnotherapist, Michael Newton, thinks soul beings select their embryos for incarnation, and once in the mother's womb, they take possession of the embryos. Newton takes hypnotized subjects beyond past lives and into soul life between lives. After numerous case studies, he concludes his patients experience a time between lives. He concludes that souls—despite being anxious to move away from the Earth—often stay for their own funerals. Guides, or those with whom they were close in previous lives, wait for souls in heaven (the spirit world). Before embarking on the journey, souls may enter a place of restoration, after which they are taken to a place of orientation, first with a guide and later with a council of elders. Spirit guides continue protective roles and, during orientation, encourage new arrivals to take responsibility for their actions on Earth. Other guides keep contact with members while they are on Earth. Occasionally, less senior guides incarnate simultaneously with their group. Some subjects have two guides, a junior still undergoing teacher training and a senior appearing less often and caring for multiple groups.

Newton's subjects report transferring to a staging area resembling a railway station, with incoming souls transiting to ethereal destinations. Many report travelling along corridors, crowded with soul groups belonging and working together in the spirit world. On joining a group, souls spend their time in the ethereal realm. The spirit world resembles a school with a multitude of classrooms under the direction of progress monitoring teachers. Because learning takes place through good natured criticism, guides become less present as groups advance. In due course, all souls have the chance to become teachers and guides. Teachings involve former lives and good and bad choices, as well as ongoing and future lessons. Most souls today are in early stages of development. Some experience two lives at the same time and can incarnate in worlds other than Earth. Subjects report communication in the ethereal realms occurring through telepathy. Private communications, though, are effected by touch, which passes between two souls as electrical sound impulses. Souls can project former life forms to communicate with other souls and, when ready, leave heaven to start another incarnation by entering an infant body.

Newton explains ghosts as discontented spirits who remain on Earth. Souls intent on harming others are secluded for remedial work and may incarnate as a victim in their next life. Rebirth into human bodies is like death, in that subjects describe travelling down a dark tunnel. Following a short delay, they find themselves in the womb. The process of assimilation with the human mind of the unborn child takes some time and must be handled carefully. Subjects enter the child's body a few months into pregnancy. In exceptional cases, incarnation is at the last minute before birth. Souls are not required to reincarnate, but spirit guides do apply considerable pressure when the time is right. Souls can choose next lives. Some choose physical disability, as it accelerates spiritual evolution. Spirits have a tendency to reincarnate in the same geographical area of past lives. Before joining a soul group as a beginner, a complete novice requires five incarnations. Novices may incarnate many times over through a lengthy Earth timespan, before advancing to intermediate status. Extreme regression, it is claimed, took a subject back to an incarnation of more than 30 000 years ago. Group placement is determined by soul level. Secondary groups have contact with primary groups. Opportunity for socialization and travel exists for souls within the group. Souls are grouped with others of similar characteristics. Souls have been reincarnating more frequently in recent centuries and, finally, souls today would have had roughly two lives during the past century.

Hybrid beings

Author and researcher David Icke equates extraterrestrials with alien spiritual beings. Stretching the imagination even further than the ideas just discussed, he introduces reptilians with both physical and spiritual characteristics. For Icke, the early root races were reptilians from other solar systems in our Milky Way Galaxy, and their status enabled them to genetically engineer humans to mine gold. Blending aliens from alternative vibratory levels with extraterrestrials from distant destinations culminated in what he calls four-dimensional aliens—beings so advanced they transcend dimensions by changing vibration.

Using the *Sumerian Tablets* and taking a literal approach, Icke says the extraterrestrials are the Anunnaki. He thinks the reptiles, having had a long connection with Earth, stretches back more than 150 million years, superseding even the dinosaurs. As with lizards and snakes they make up one of the reptilian streams in this universe. The reptiles and dinosaurs were closely related in appearance and have spawned a variety of forms. The diversity of the reptile-dinosaur stream made it possible for them to manifest in two-legged, two-armed forms with the brain capacity for technically advanced consciousness.

Icke asks if the evolutionary leap from dinosaurs to reptilian humanoids did not happen in another dimension or planet, or perhaps on Earth before the demise of the dinosaurs. Were they in fact eliminated? Although the dinosaurs disappeared, their consciousness may have been retained. Consciousness is energy, and although it can be transmuted into different forms, it cannot be destroyed. He sees a resemblance between some dinosaurs and depictions of ancient dragons. The dinosaur consciousness, which dominated the Earth a million years ago, survived, evolving into conscious spirit race with reptilian characteristics. Although he does not go as far as to say the Anunnaki reptilians originated from the dinosaurs, he draws parallels between the two, postulating that they could be linked. Millions of years later, after occupying most of the galaxy or universe, they returned to Earth, creating havoc.

Icke believes an Anunnaki-human crossbreed elite, which interbred extraterrestrials and humans, are the gods or sky people of the Sumerian texts. He writes of gods from other worlds interbreeding with humanity, creating a hybrid network of bloodlines, and he believes the serpent from the biblical Garden of Eden originated in Sumer. The reptilians claimed the divine right of kings; the God-given right to rule. The bloodlines gave rise to the royal and aristocratic families of Europe and, thanks to the British Empire and the other European empires, were exported to the Americas, Africa, Australia, New Zealand, and across into the Far East, where they connected with hybrid bloodlines in China. Icke also thinks the hybrids became the political and economic rulers of the European empires. The United States houses millions of people from the diverse genetic pool. Forty-two American presidents were related. Thirty-three can be traced to Charlemagne, the celebrated monarch of France. The Charlemagne lineage features strongly in the bloodline expansion from Britain, France, and Germany. And finally, the reptilians control the entire planet.

For Icke, the origins for the Anunnaki intervention are threefold: *extraterrestrials* from the Draco star constellation; *inner terrestrials* living within Earth; and *other dimensional reptilians* with human bodies manipulating humanity from the lower-fourth dimension. Like tuning a radio or changing channels on a television, other dimensional creatures transmigrate from one vibration or dimension to another. Although many other dimensions exist, humans are mostly tuned to the third. Human consciousness can be tuned to other wavelengths and connected with information on alternative frequencies. This is the basic principle of psychic power, and it is from one of these realities that the Anunnaki control the world, infiltrating bloodline streams.

Icke thinks the reptilians are themselves controlled by fifth-dimensional entities. The non-physical reptilians poured into our dimension through portals in the time-space caused by nuclear testing, which started in New Mexico in the early 1940s. The reptilians are between five and twelve feet tall and have wings like flaps of skin supported by ribs, which fold back against the body. The cape of Count Dracula is symbolic of these wings. The Draco are also known as the Dragon Race. Some are white or albino, not the usual green or brown. The Draco are the royalty of reptilians, with the highest caste being the albinos with conical horns midway between the brow and the top of the skull. Other species, like the soldier class and scientists, are known as Reptoids. They do not have wings, but all are cold-blooded. The scales on their backs are much larger and they have three fingers with an opposing thumb, and three toes with a fourth towards the side of the ankle and short, blunt claws. They have large, cat-like eyes that glow red and a slit for a mouth. Some have black eyes and others are white with flame-colored vertical pupils.

*****

The immaterial soul that requires a body of sorts dates to the second-century Christian prelate of the Church,

Irenaeus. Attributing a certain corporeal character to the soul, he describes it as taking on the form of its body, just as water takes on the form of its containing vessel. Nearly two thousand years later, Newton's idea of souls projecting former lives and appearing as a mass of energy recapitulates Irenaeus's corporeal souls. The question of whether the soul is material, immaterial, or can change to variant stages in between is therefore not resolved. There, against Von Daniken's idea of a mothership with extraterrestrials cruising into our solar system, begs the question regarding the soul. Human origination from extraterrestrials and/or alien spiritual beings does not make sense. Would aliens such as these, capable of engineering slaves, create them empowered with a spiritual component such as the soul? Surely the soul empowers Earthlings beyond death and serves no purpose for the creators.

Awarding corporeality to the soul has always been tempting, but the sentiment lacks credibility. The soul is either material or it is immaterial—which means exactly that, no matter, and therefore no color to radiate. Its cyclical migration also implies the soul is intrinsically parasitic, needing a host every time it enters the physical realm. Alien souls acting as parasites, invading embryos in the wombs of unsuspecting mothers, is too ghastly to contemplate. Imagine Adolph Hitler reincarnating through a loving mother. Surely, the mother should have a say as to what she allows into her womb (souls apparently fight over embryos). People believing souls choose parents also believe in good or evil. Pools of souls waiting for life to evolve before entering the bodies of *Homo sapiens* also sound farfetched. What were they doing all that time? Do they become tired of incarnating? What if they do not like the environment or the parents? Is that baby born without a soul? After all, the souls hung around for eons before entering human bodies. Who can these souls be, or where can they possibly come from before making the miraculous inception into the embryo? Did they hang around with a God? Are they from purgatory? Do they escape from heaven or hell? The questions are limitless.

Then, there is the question of the Reptilian Anunnaki invading the Earth. With a degree in Ancient History and Egyptology, David Rohl has a simpler view. For him, the Anunnaki were those who came from heaven (*an*) to settle on earth (*ki*)—people who came from the mountains to the alluvial plains. They were mortal men who became earthbound gods of flesh and blood, passing from the mortal world to govern the underworld of the dead. They did not dwell among the *Igigi* gods of heaven. The Egyptians also knew them as the mythological founders of civilization, the revered *Shebtiu*, or the Senior Ones. Throughout history, heaven has been synonymous with high grounds or mountainous areas. Controlling the high ground had great significance. Dominance in a time of war was gained through control over the high ground, and during times of floods and catastrophe, one's survival depended on it.

Lyall Watson, author of *Supernature 1* and *Supernature 2*, thinks it is the cluster of semi-normal phenomena existent between normal occurrences and those which are impossible to explain, which falls in the arena of supernature. Humans have a need to believe in the unseen, and even though this may have merit, the question arises whether this is a part of our character or whether things unseen exist. As studies about the occult increase, more will be revealed. With so many reports of supernatural experiences, it is difficult to dismiss the unexplained. For Watson, the supernatural needs a new, fresh, and thorough overview—a system designed to retrieve, catalogue, and classify unusual events. Altogether, nothing is supernatural; it is only we that make it so.

Chapter 5

Materialism

How does spirituality face up to the scientific and philosophical models of today? Simply, it does not. The new scientific model barely provides for free will, either. Despite progress in neurology, the relationship of the brain to thought, emotion, reason, desire, and memory is yet unexplained. And although the Cartesian model links the soul with consciousness, the scientific and philosophical models are unable to confirm whether the mind is physical or non-physical. Both philosophical and neurobiological views are influenced by materialism, which denies the existence of the soul. Materialism holds that existence is a characteristic or consequence of matter. Matter is the elemental component of reality, and physio-chemical changes in the nervous system of the brain are the ultimate source of consciousness. The more the activity of neurons and synapses is understood, the less believable is a "ghost" controlling the machine. Since the introduction of Charles

Darwin's theory of evolution, materialism has largely embraced the principles in which primacy of mind is affirmed and matter defined as one of its characteristics.

Many believe materialism succeeds where idealism (all reality is but an idea) and neutral monism (reality is neither exclusively mental nor solely physical) fails in credibility. Materialism presents in various forms, each with its stumbling blocks, the most daunting being that it seems nearly impossible for people to discard spiritual experience and attribute it to an illusion of the mind. People conceive of the soul as the inner self, which survives death. Nevertheless, as Blackmore points out, there is no separate stuff called the soul, and if someone did make this discovery, it would be incorporated into the physical. If the soul cannot be identified as a physical entity, it is difficult to see how it could control the brain.

Owen Flanagan, professor of philosophy at Duke University in Durham, North Carolina, deals with the conflict between the humanistic and the scientific views— the two predominant images of the structure of humans. According to the humanistic image, humans are spiritual beings empowered with free will, which permits them to outsmart the laws of cause and effect. The scientific image differs, claiming that humans are animals evolving via the principle of natural selection. Although they are extraordinary animals, they do not have the capacity to transcend the laws of cause and effect. Which concept is closer to the truth: humanism or science? The two views seem incompatible. But could both be right?

Humanism holds that humans have a spiritual aspect with an incorporeal mind (or soul), with life and fate determined by the state of this soul. Science decrees that humans are social animals and ultimately mortal, and since there is no soul or eternal life, they cannot take comfort from the luxury of a soul. The humanistic image includes a non-physical mind with free will and a lasting soul that is changeless. This view is rejected by science, which views the soul as old-fashioned, dismissing it as a belief held only by intransigent believers.

Flanagan asserts the humanistic view is flawed by two errors: that mind is disembodied and that will can be free. How does a non-physical mind cause a body to move? The Cartesian idea of free will relies on mental events, and choice is the motivator of material life. If one rejects the idea that the mental and physical interact, being impossible to explain such a mechanism, it follows one must reject the Cartesian definition of free will, since it relies on that fundamental principle.

Leibniz originally overcame the problem with his philosophy that God created the universe with a set plan for each person's mind and body to function synchronistically. Malebranche believes there is no interaction and it is God who causes the mind and body to interact in harmony. This parallelism is compatible with determinism in that it denies the existence of free will. Flanagan rejects the theories of both Leibniz and Malebranche; he even rejects Cartesian dualism and accepts the naturalistic mind, in which free will remains undetermined until fully understanding the nature of that which governs mind. He thinks the mind and brain may work in a way yet to be discovered, which is not deterministic and which resembles the Cartesian idea of free will. This open-ended approach is rejected by science, which claims all are animals and the brain is the mind.

As in science, Flanagan asserts that the mind derives from the brain. Consciousness, cognition, and volition are abilities of humans that enable them to cope with the complexity of the natural and social environments. Humans have no special capabilities to do the work of the mind, soul, or free will. *Desouling* is a requirement of the scientific image; it is mandatory to discard the soul and non-physical mind. Their existence would render science unable to explain people; consequently, the soul does not exist and people can be explained scientifically. Furthermore, people are natural creatures, obedient and responsive to natural law, as befits our physical nature. Religion, which places humans between animals on the one hand, and with angels and God on the other, needs to be replaced by a rational belief system. Although complex and unusual, humans are, nonetheless, animals. Thus, science is committed to desouling all animals, including humans.

Agreeing with science, Flanagan claims there is no spiritual component and that the attainment of perfection within the constraints of the scientific model should be encouraged. We are in the age of mind-science in which cognitive science and neuroscience are using reliable tools to identify the workings of the mind/brain. The brain and nervous system comprise the thinking self. The scientific model concludes that humans are conscious animals living at a certain time in the landscape of natural and social history. Flanagan clarifies the assumptions of the scientific image: the mind is the brain and the mind is obedient to natural law, which is causal. In the first instance, mental events are brain events or, more specifically, mental events are central nervous system events, even whole person events. The mind evolves per evolutionary principles, and there is no free will.

Humanism questions the scientific view, seeing it as dehumanizing and draining life of meaning. For Flanagan, the absence of the soul is acceptable. Both models share a similar goal: to maintain a clear concept of what it means to be a person with consciousness, the capacity for self-knowledge and the ability to live rationally, morally, and meaningfully. Flanagan thinks the humanistic image, whereby the soul reigns supreme, should be discarded. Even without souls, non-physical minds, immutable selves, or free will, humans are still people. The scientific view is sometimes seen as negative, since it has not demonstrated the difference between animal and human. For some, acceptance of evolution renders life meaningless and removes purpose from the universe. At the heart of this thought lies nihilism, with its idea that something without purpose has no meaning.

Flannigan finally holds that, although Darwin demonstrated that evolution of species is unplanned, this does not imply that life *has* no meaning or purpose. Even though evolution spawned intelligence, it does not follow that intelligence is needed to bring it about. Evolution has produced meaning. We have language, words, and signs, all of which have meaning. It is a common mistake to think that evolution negates meaning and purpose. Evolution is a process through which lifeforms, behaviors, and consciousness emerge. There is no need for a God to give life meaning and purpose, and that includes the existence of an afterlife.

Chapter 6

Triunism

Despite the influence of science and philosophy in denuding humanity of its soul, the soul remains integral to the self-image of billions worldwide. For too long, the deep-rooted impression that the soul guarantees immortality has offered that the earthly sojourn is not in vain. But are those who believe in the existence of the soul deluded? It is comforting to conceive of the soul as a vehicle for consciousness beyond material death. But is this realistic?

It would be impossible to include a critique of everything ever written about the soul, and the doctrines that incorporate the soul have rarely been challenged. I am attempting here to show how little we know of the soul. However, some expositions do invite exploration. As scientific knowledge of the cosmos expands, together with ongoing evolution, the further those of scientific bent move away from acknowledging the spiritual nature. Yet that is exactly where the answer lies. The pertinent question should be: at which point in the evolutionary process did humans acquire souls capable of a spiritual life?

To establish whether we are empowered with a soul, we need a fresh view. Concepts of the soul in our contemporary world need to be compatible with scientific models describing the origin of the universe and evolution of life on Earth. There is a respectable body of evidence demonstrating the existence of the universe for over nearly 14 billion years, with evolutionary life on Earth taking place over 3.5 billion years. There is abundant evidence of genus *Homo* evolving over the past two million years. During this process, at what point did the soul arrive?

Perhaps equating the mind with the soul is misdirected. Evolution implies that the soul is a changing entity and that perceptions must also change. The *Gospel of Matthew* credits Jesus with saying that humans are possessed of a heart, soul, and mind. Was Jesus right? If he was, and humans have a heart, soul, and mind, it would present a new type of alliance. And that triune alliance I name *Triunism*.

Triunism is the concept where a living organism has a material body, a cognitive brain function, and an added spiritual component of a separable soul. The cognitive brain is electro-chemical, resulting from neurological activity carrying electrical charges by way of chemical interactions. In addition, humans have a soul-mind, presently expressed through the subconscious, which is connected to alternative dimensions and realities. And yes, the soul nature can exist outside of, and perhaps independently of, the physical body. But no, the soul is not the mind itself; it is the vehicle for this mind. However, I am not convinced that the soul is immortal—yet. Triunism, therefore, holds that humans are physical beings in *two minds*, so to speak—a state of being brought about by eons of evolution.

Even if not proven yet, it is clear the mind is a product of the brain. Neurobiology shows that cognizance and memory stop when the brain dies. Nevertheless, this does not mean that soul and soul-mind are not capable of surviving biological death. There is reason to acknowledge that humans have another mind at work, in some respects, capable of outperforming the brain-mind. What would constitute proof of a soul-mind independent of the brain-mind? If we can detect a consciousness beyond the confines of the brain and its mind, that would surely be grounds for the existence of soul-mind at a distance, so to speak. This, of course, is the reason why humans believe in a soul—they do experience consciousness outside the confines of the physical body.

The idea of the astral counterpart as a vehicle for consciousness outside the material body, as proclaimed in occultism, warrants investigation. Astral projection is the ability to project consciousness and visual perception while remaining linked to the body by way of a *silver cord*. Bruce Roberts in *Astral Dynamics* describes the mind split during astral projection, also known as out of body experience (OBE). Despite the body being left alone when the astral double exits, Roberts thinks that some consciousness is still present. There is disagreement whether it is the astral body or the etheric which separates. Considering that the etheric body is the life-giving force of the material body, as previously mentioned, it is unlikely it could leave the body without precipitating the death of the latter.

Roberts thinks consciousness reflects a copy of itself outside the body. The reflection into an energetic vehicle capable of supporting and maintaining its integrity outside the body is a kind of energetic copy of consciousness, mind, and memory. The body is never empty and unprotected, and the blueprint of consciousness does not leave the boundaries of the body. During sleep or trance, consciousness projects into the etheric body and another full copy of consciousness and memory is reflected onto it. The moment of separation, when the body projects, is when the first true mind split occurs. The process results in two energetic copies, plus a master copy of consciousness and memory.

Near death experiences (NDEs), where people experience sensations shortly after death, has also fascinated researchers for some time. Dr. Bruce Greyson, professor of psychiatry and a member of the Parapsychological Association, has gathered empirical data on NDEs for decades. His *Weighted Core Experience Index* and *Near-Death Experience Scale* measures the depth and explores the veracity of NDEs. The Greyson scale reflects the following sixteen features: experience of an altered state of time, accelerated thought, review of life, a sense of sudden understanding, feelings of peace, joy and cosmic oneness, seeing light or being surrounded by it, vivid sensations, extrasensory perception, visions, a sense of being out of the physical body, a sense of an otherworldly environment, a sense of a mystical entity, a sense of deceased and/or religious figures, and the experience of a point of no return.

J. Timothy Green, in *Near Death Experiences, Shamanism, and the Scientific Method*, documents shamans entering an altered state at will. Numerous methods are used, but the most frequent are fasting, floral potions, or prolonged drumming. The shaman, on achieving an ecstatic state, enters an extraordinary reality, which precipitates travel to other realms for a specific purpose. Green documents how shamanic cosmology postulates three distinct but interpenetrating realms, which are experienced as real but different from physical reality. Shamans enter altered states using their minds. They become active participants capable of developing and maintaining relationships with the beings of that realm. Since they habitually visit this realm, shamans become familiar with the geography and its inhabitants. Shamans believe that all things are endowed with spirit: animals, plants, and even minerals.

Astral projection can only stand as evidence for the individual whose experience it is. Lacking scientific verification, one could posit that astral projection is a hallucination. Skeptics note that the brain can mimic OBEs. Professor and neurologist Olaf Blanke and his colleagues at Geneva University Hospital in Switzerland, bring about OBEs through electrical stimulation of the brain. On occasion, people have found themselves exiting their bodies, observing life from an exterior vantage point. Neurologists found that stimulation of the angular gyrus in the right cortex precipitated OBEs. With increased current, the person experiences leaving the body. Patients have seen themselves from above, looking down at their own bodies. Professor Blanke believes the angular gyrus is responsible for the duplication of visual information.

Medical researchers are looking for proof that consciousness can exit the body and observe life from outside. Studies so far suggest that consciousness can survive death and that the mind and brain are distinct from one another. On 15 December 2001, the respected international medical journal, *The Lancet*, published an article by Pim van Lommel, Ruud van Wees, Vincent Meyers, and Ingrid Elfferich. The report: *Near-death experience in survivors of cardiac arrest: a prospective study in the Netherlands*, recounts how 12% of 344 cardiac patients resuscitated from clinical death described NDEs. Some patients experienced a sensation of being out of body, while others experienced the familiar light at the end of a tunnel. Skeptics assert that these events are hallucinations stimulated by loss of oxygen to the brain as the heart stops beating.

The results of Van Lommel, who headed the investigation, show that NDEs cannot be explained by medical factors alone. Cardiac arrest means patients are clinically dead, with unconsciousness resulting from insufficient blood supply to the brain. When this happens, the electroencephalogram (EEG), which measures the brain's electrical activity, shows up as flattened, and the patient—without cardiopulmonary resuscitation (CPR) within five to ten minutes—is likely to suffer irreparable brain damage or death. Accepting that NDE is caused by anoxia, then all the patients in their study should have had similar NDEs. Van Lommel thinks NDEs are caused by psychological states induced by the fear of death. Only a percentage experienced fear directly before cardiac arrest. For most, the cardiac arrest happened so quickly they had no time for fear. Of the survivors, 18% had memory recall, 12% had a significant experience, and 6% a superficial one. Scientists noted that NDE patients recalled their experience with the same degree of detail when interviewed again several years later.

Several theories are aimed at rationalizing NDEs. Since stimulation of areas of the cortex can induce NDE-like experiences, this suggests that neurophysiological processes must play a part. Experimenters with drugs such as ketamine, LSD, and psychedelic mushrooms have also induced NDEs, but the recollections are fragmented and random. Another opinion is that the NDE is a changing state of consciousness in which memories, identity, cognition, and emotion function independently from the body through retained non-sensory perception.

The determining factor for establishing an OBE lies in ascertaining whether the brain is dead at the time of the event. If the brain is shown to be clinically dead by a flattened EEG, there is no chance of the mind functioning to produce thought. For Van Lommel, the events raise medical concepts about the range of human consciousness and the mind-brain relationship to new possibilities. Some patients, although shown to be clinically dead, report consciousness and cognitive functions such as emotion, identity, memory from early childhood, and perceptions from a position out of and above their "dead" bodies. Clinically dead, in this context, means the brain has no electrical activity in the cortex, with total loss of brain stem function evidenced by fixed, dilated pupils and absence of the gag reflex. How can coherent thought occur when the brain is dead?

These studies challenge the traditional view that thought, consciousness, and memory are produced by groups of neurons in the brain. Van Lommel finds it paradoxical that coherence and logical thought are possible under cerebrally impaired conditions, and this raises puzzling questions about our understanding of consciousness and its relationship to brain function.

University of Southampton researchers have published a paper detailing the study of NDEs that also suggests consciousness after the brain has ceased to function and the body is clinically dead. The team spent a year studying people revived after suffering a heart attack. The patients were clinically dead, with no pulse, no respiration, and with fixed, dilated pupils. EEG studies conclusively confirmed that all electrical brain activity had ceased. After resuscitation, 11% of surviving patients recalled emotions and visions during the period of clinical death. Seven survivors interviewed within a week of cardiac arrest reported NDEs. Four complied with the strict Greyson criteria used to diagnose NDEs.

Dr. Parnia, a clinical researcher from Southampton General Hospital in England, suggests these findings about the experience of dying and the nature of mind during the process need further investigation. If the results can be replicated, this would surely confirm that the mind continues to exist after death. Broadly, three scientific points of view exist: patients hallucinate; psychological factors exist to ease the process of death; and the soul continues consciousness, confirming life after death.

A powerful example of consciousness beyond the brain comes from cardiologist, Dr. Michael Sabom, whose book, *Light and Death*, includes a case study of Pam Reynolds, who underwent a rare operation to remove a life-threatening basilar arterial aneurysm in her brain. The size and location of the aneurysm made standard neurosurgical techniques impossible. Nicknamed *standstill*, the operation reduced the body temperature to sixty degrees, stopped the heartbeat and breathing, brain waves were flattened, and blood was drained from the head. In other words, Pam was put to death. In no circumstance should anyone experience consciousness during such an operation.

Three clinical tests were performed to determine whether Pam's brain was clinically dead during her operation. The standard EEG measured wave activity, auditory evoked potentials measured brain-stem viability, and blockage of blood flow to the brain was complete. Pam's EEG was silent, her brain-stem response was absent, and no blood flowed through her brain. After removing the aneurysm, Pam was restored to life. During the operation, however, Pam experienced a NDE and gave detailed observations of what took place during surgery. She even described unique surgical instruments and procedures used in the operation. The phenomenon does not stop there. All Pam's vital signs were stopped and her skull was cut open. She reported herself popping outside her body and hovering above the operating table. She watched doctors working on her lifeless body and observed them using a tiny saw similar to an electric toothbrush. She reported conversations among the theatre staff and recalled all stages of the operation. During this time, every monitor used to register life showed that Pam was indeed dead. Pam's case study is one of the strongest examples of evidence for NDEs to date.

To say NDEs provide evidence for the soul's existence in other dimensions or spiritual realms is premature. Scientists probing the paranormal are hoping to set up further experiments to determine with more accuracy whether the mind can step outside the body at the threshold of death. Triunism postulates that it is not the mind of the brain, but a secondary mind of the soul, which can separate from the body. This implies the existence of two minds and perhaps even consciousness—a rational mind function and a spiritual soul function. The brain and its thoughts operate in the physical dimension and the soul-mind in an alternative realm. There are those who imagine themselves having such abilities, enabling them to tap into both minds at will. The problem with this is that some subjects tend to manifest schizophrenic episodes. In a way, the concept of operating in two minds has become familiar for those who can think with one mind, at the same time assessing those thoughts with a secondary mind. It is likened to being conscious of consciousness or being in two minds.

The concept of triunism—body, mind, and soul—is not new. For thousands of years, humans have experienced God communicating with them through the Holy Spirit. Others have guides or experience angelic visitations. Perhaps this is the soul-mind interacting with the brain-mind. Perhaps the soul passing information to the mind. The soul is getting a mind of its own. This is the feeling of being in two minds.

Chapter 7

Cosmic Soul

Souls are not found in the observable universe. If the soul does exist, it is not seen in our dimensions of space and time. We like to hope each person has a soul. How does one recognize something that cannot be apprehended either with our sensory perception or with any of our cunningly devised instruments?

The highest attribute of the human, which supersedes all other life forms, is consciousness of our own consciousness. Humans have considerable understanding of their thought processes and existence; we have the gift of consciousness and to be simultaneously aware of this gift. But this was not always the case.

Homo sapiens date from 150 000 to 200 000 years ago; preceding them were *Australopithecus* and primates. Evolution did not cease with *Homo sapiens*; humans are, of course, subject to evolution—a process that has always been considered biological. What if humans also evolve on a spiritual level? What if the soul is a product of evolution? Why, in the first place, did humans come to believe in the soul?

The creationist view of God creating heaven and Earth in six days is challenged by discoveries that the universe is around 13.8 billion years old and that life on Earth has already existed for more than 3.5 billion years. At which point in these eons of time did the soul appear? The soul requires three elements: life, the *ego* or I, and a consciousness free of the material body. Contemporary science may throw some light on this perplexing issue.

Scientists claim that the universe is the consequence of the massive explosion known as the Big Bang. The American astronomer Edwin Hubble, in the nineteen-twenties, produced evidence that the universe is expanding, when he observed clusters of galaxies moving apart from one another. This expansion was also predicted in the early twentieth century by Albert Einstein in the general theory of relativity. How creation initially came into being is still beyond our knowledge. Theories of cosmic origin and evolution throw light on the origins and current state of the universe. Technology, such as telescopes, microscopes, and particle oscillators, facilitate observation of the inner and outer fabric of the cosmic environment. X-rays, computerized axial tomography (CAT scans), magnetic resonance imagery (MRI), and positron emission tomography (PET), give insight into the bodies of living creatures. These technologies are devised to overcome the limitations of the human senses and these instruments allow humans to observe and understand the environment we live in. Yet, despite all the technological advances, we cannot identify the soul.

The Big Bang theory establishes that primary forces and fundamental particles constituting the building blocks of the universe were already present in the first split second after the big bang. About one ten-thousandth of a second after this event, the temperature of the universe reached around one thousand billion degrees Celsius. As the universe cooled and expanded, the photons and particle matter lost energy, rendering them interchangeable. Observed as background radiation, the subsidence of the universe into stable matter is still observed today with advanced telescopes. Estimates are that the vital materials of the cosmos had already formed by the end of the first second, while stars and galaxies had another million years to wait before forming. A cooling process accompanied the expansion from its earliest state, until two hundred and fifty million years later, when the universe had cooled to a chilling one hundred degrees below freezing. With the lower temperatures—marked by the critical level at which the density of ordinary matter becomes greater than the mass density of radiant energy—the possibility of life emerged.

The transition from the dominance of radiation to that of matter altered the behavior of matter so that, with the help of gravity, it became dominant. This crucial event determined the freedom of matter from radiant energy. Gas spread evenly and formed massive clouds, which eventually drifted apart as the universe continued to expand. This same gas formed the stars and galaxies. For another billion years, the galaxies and planets took shape, during which time water, ammonia, nitrogen, oxygen, and a few other elements that constitute life also emerged. Several billion years later, there are trillions of stars and billions of spiraling galaxies, solar systems, and planets, including Earth, which formed around five billion years ago.

The universe measures approximately 30 billion light years across, which means it would take light travelling at the speed of 300 000 km/sec. (187 000 miles/sec.), 30 billion years to cover the distance from one side of the universe to the other. A light year is about 9.6 trillion kilometers—the distance light travels in a year. This is massive! Beyond this, humans cannot see. Some theoretical scientists are speculating many other universes may be forming a multiverse.

Humans do not live long enough to make space travel on an intergalactic scale viable. The physics of our day does not allow for inter-solar space travel, let alone intergalactic migration. The biggest obstacle is not so much the physics, but our physio-chemical bodies. Even if humans could live long enough, our bodies are unable to withstand the harsh conditions in space to allow space travel over long distances. The Earthly body only lasts about a hundred years, and travelling constantly for this period will hardly get us out of our own solar system, let alone to the nearest neighboring sun. Either humans must find faster ways to travel through space, or they must live longer. That brings us to the mass factor. Bodies have mass and mass is difficult to project into and through space.

There is no purpose in searching for soul prior to the advent of life. There is no knowledge of life existing prior to 3.8 billion years ago. British scientist Charles Darwin, whose work has had an extraordinary effect on our perception of life, discovered how all forms of life are subject to a process of evolution through natural selection. His theory introduced the idea that man once belonged to the primate family and that our ancestors were apes. In the theory of common descent, he shows that all living organisms are derived from common ancestors and that all ultimately have *one* common ancestor in the form of a single solitary bacterium dating 3,8 billion years ago. Micro-organisms found in sedimentary rocks at Barberton, South Africa date from around that time. Receiving energy from the sun enabled them to produce oxygen, which they released into the atmosphere. Yet, it is only two centuries since the humans discovered evolution.

Whether bacteria or primate, life exists only in the tiny biosphere extending a mere 10 km (6 miles) around the surface of Earth. Unless of course we include spaceships or stations orbiting the Earth, there is no other known destination supporting life. There may be other functional biospheres in the universe, but we have yet to find them.

Life either emerged from a single cell or group of organisms from the same species of cells from which all life on Earth descended. One of the first accounts of living matter originating from lifeless matter and its ability to perform continuous evolutionary processes was introduced in the mid-twentieth century by the Russian biochemist, Alexander Oparin. Initially called molecular evolution, it is now more commonly referred to as pre-biotic evolution. Despite the idea of pre-biotic evolution having aspects that are still speculative, biologists and biochemists do not doubt that life originated on Earth as a result of a sequence of chemical events, allowing the abundance of forms of plant and animal to spring from a single ancestor.

Bearing in mind that we are still looking for the first requirement (life) for the soul to exist, it behooves us to examine life. The term life applies to the activity of all organisms—plants, animals, bacteria, and even viruses. Primitive forms—the simplest of living systems—consist of a basic structure of one cell. All life in organisms manifests characteristics of reproduction and evolution. The first act of life is to reproduce by making identical or near identical copies of itself. The second characteristic of life is to change and increase the complexity of form and nature through gradual evolutionary modification. The third requirement for life is the need for an organic structure with enough energy for the processes to take place.

Bacteria are single-celled and separated from the environment by a thin semi-permeable membrane; plants and animals are multi-cellular. All living organisms use metabolic processes to produce a constant flow of matter and energy in their cellular network to repair and replace their structure. An organism is never in equilibrium, and when new structures seemingly spontaneously emerge, we are witnessing evolution in action. The genetic instructions for building a cell or multi-cellular organisms are written in a chemical code or genome composed of nucleic acid. It is usually RNA (ribonucleic acid) that is the genetic carrying messenger. DNA (deoxyribonucleic acid) stores the genetic information and is responsible for the self-replication of the cell. DNA is the memory of the species and is copied and transmitted to each generation. The molecular structure of DNA is a double helix wound together. Reproduction of the genome takes place when the DNA's double helix separates and a new strand is created alongside each of the original strands, resulting in two identical DNA molecules.

Even though DNA is material in nature and made up of atoms as are all physical objects it is thought, as per divine design, to carry the message of life and form. The message of the simplest free-living bacteria is written in the genome of about two thousand genes, whereas human DNA requires billions of atoms.

Even though life can be explained in minute detail, right from the first bacteria, we still cannot say what caused the initial cell to make its appearance. The second unexplained (and therefore supernatural) event is the inception of life with the forming of the first cell. Was there a god's hand at work? Evolution postulates that all life is descended from a single clone. The origin of life is a mystery, and scientists are unable to explain how the very first microbe came into existence—chance or divine intervention. Since science does not allow for mystical speculation, it chooses chance.

Is there a mind behind a DNA string able to replicate itself and evolve? What instructs the atoms in basic forms of life such as viruses and bacteria to form and perform in the way they do? Do organisms that display autonomous behavior and that can replicate and evolve require a life-giving force or a soul to live? Science says no—life happens spontaneously and is self-generated. Any explanation of how life came into existence and how it is sustained is illusory and cannot be explained. No properly conducted experiment has ever demonstrated a life force. Science will not recognize a mystical ingredient. In seeking to understand the origin of life, science looks to molecular processes to explain live matter, not to any external force. But is there a consciousness that informs life? In religious contexts, God is the giver of life. Despite science rejecting the notion of informed life, it is worth exploring.

Occultists hold there is an invisible (to ordinary sight) intermediate realm between the divine and the physical realm with life-generating attributes informing life in the physical realm. The idea of quintessence is given to a formative energy, which gives structure to the environment. The Greek philosopher, Empedocles, in the fourth century BC, thought that all things are formed of the four primal elements of earth, air, fire, and water. Aristotle sketched the universe as spherical and finite, made up of the four elements. Occultism describes five cosmic elements, the fifth being the elusive component, quintessence, which is the element binding the other four (some systems include Buddhi and Atma).

Quintessence has many names: *aether*, *akasha*, *akasa*, *akasia*, or *akashya*. Blavatsky characterized *aether* as a cosmically radiant, cool, diathermal plastic matter, creative in its physical nature. In theosophy, it is the luminous fifth element, the binding element of the other four. In early occultism, it was known as luminous or mercurial waters. Contemporary occultism calls it the cosmic memory. In occult lore, quintessence is the fifth element of seven—the sixth and seventh being even more elusive than quintessence. It is widely recognized that quintessence is visible to clairvoyants and will, in the future, become visible to most humans.

Apart from the elements of earth, air, water, and fire, for which occultism sees quintessence as the binding element, a further etheric force exists as the life-giving force of organisms. The etheric level exists between the physical and the psychic world. Etheric forces work on inert matter to produce the rich diversity of plants, animals, and humans; the cycles of nature; and much of the planetary phenomena observed from Earth. All life is imbued with etheric energy, and the quality of life depends on its nature within a given being. The etheric double is a delicate body, which penetrates the physical body and suspends it in the state called life. The human etheric double is slightly larger than the physical body. Informing the etheric is the life-giving astral force, which exists at a higher vibration. The astral creates a replica, which transmits into the physical dimension and manifests as a material object. In occultism, the etheric body is the minimum requirement for life in any organism. The spiritual counterpart is the astral body, and its memory is the equivalent of quintessence for the physical body. When the etheric is withdrawn, the body becomes inert and disintegrates into its constituent elements.

At its most fundamental, science claims that organisms do not require spiritual forces, such as etheric or astral. Nonetheless, some scientists are renewing their interest in this area; the reason being the discovery that we live in an ever-expanding universe. Prior to the close of the twentieth century, the thinking was that the expansion was decelerating because of gravitation, but then the opposite was found to be true. As if propelled by an unknown force greater than gravitation, galaxies are driven apart at increasing acceleration. Measurements of supernova and cosmic microwave background show that the universe is flat and will expand forever. This is a mystery, because the belief was that there could not be enough substance to build a flat universe. This image of the universe implies that undiscovered components of dark matter and dark energy exist and are largely responsible for the way the universe evolves. Since no one has been able to examine this elusive matter, there is no knowledge of its structure. It is more prevalent than ordinary matter, and evidence suggests that more than two-thirds of the universe is invisible due to our inability to observe all elements of physical reality.

Cosmologists propose that the acceleration is related to quintessence. Perhaps dark matter and energy are science's equivalent of quintessence? Various ongoing experiments will provide the key to this hypothesis and offer fresh insight into the nature of the universe. Dark energy was a mathematical absurdity not so long ago, and physicists need now to explore the nature of quintessence before proposing a unified theory of the fundamental forces. So, what is dark matter and energy and how does it relate to quintessence? In the 1930s, quantum physicists discovered, much to their surprise, that no vacuum is ever truly empty. It is buzzing with activity, filled with particles and energy, and that "empty space" is in fact a complex substance. Now, there is a pressing need to gain knowledge of dark matter and energy, for it may well be the dark essence found in the vacuum and everywhere else in the universe is the force propelling expansion.

Surprisingly, this is what mystics have been saying for thousands of years: that empty space is anything but empty. Clairvoyants are bombarded with animated visual textures and spiritual forces in what was thought to be empty space. Quintessence, as a formative force that is visible to clairvoyant occultists, may be a reality.

After billions of years of evolution of life on Earth, humans are at the forefront of the process. Humans evolved thought and consciousness and with that came the realization of the dangers involved in life on Earth. Hence the need to plan against the dangers. One of the long-term goals to overcome the limitations of life on Earth is to seek new frontiers. New frontiers in science today are mostly focused on alternative destinations in our solar system and hopefully to other solar systems beyond. Space travel could perhaps be available for the select few, but ultimately it would be a dead end. What then? What if spirituality is closer to the truth? What if we have been looking at spirituality in the wrong way? What if spirituality is a destination, not a religion? What could provide a playground for the elusive soul nature? Will science embrace a dash of occultism to provide a dwelling place for the spiritual nature we call our soul?

Chapter 8

Consciousness

Evolution teaches that *Homo sapiens* share a common ancestor, which can be traced back to the family of primates still existing today. Chimpanzees are the closest relatives of humans. Research shows that certain enzymes and proteins taken from humans and chimpanzees are virtually identical. Asymmetries in the left and right hemispheres of the brain of chimpanzees resemble that of modern humans. Chimpanzees and humans share more than 98% of their DNA and 99% of their genes, showing how closely related they are; indeed, chimpanzees are more closely related to humans than to their nearest primate cousin, the orangutans. Remember, no two humans have the same genes.

Living from around seven million years ago, the earliest human-like apes, the Australopithecines, walked in an upright position. All six species had relatively small brains and ape-like proportions. These primates probably developed bipedal locomotion to adapt to new habitats, although they remained tree dwellers, sleeping in tree nests like other apes. About 2.5 million years ago, the Earth's climate was transformed by a change in its axis. As the planet spun away from the sun, it precipitated cooling and climates developed seasons. The lower temperatures resulted in the destruction of tracts of woodland, leaving belts of savannah in its place. Some animals suffered extinction, while others evolved.

The Australopithecines comprised two groups: the heavier-built *Australopithecus aethiopicus*, *A. robustus*, and *A. boisei*, who roamed the Earth around 2.5 to 1 million years ago and ate vegetable matter, and the lighter framed *A. afarensis*, *A. garhi*, and *A. africanus* of 3.7 to 2 million years ago, whose diet was more extensive. Evidence suggests the *A. africanus* evolved into the genus *Homo*—the family of man.

Fossil remains show us the oldest *Homo* species, *Homo habilis*. Living around two million years ago, they were the first human-like beings to use stone tools. *Homo erectus* may have survived in parts of Asia long after the species died out elsewhere. They were more robust than *Homo habilis*, with larger brains. There is controversy as to whether all *Homo* fossils from this time can be attributed to this single species. It is thought that *Homo erectus* spread from Africa to Asia between 1.9 and 1.7 million years ago and was the first to extend further into Africa. Their fossils have been found from eastern Asia and Java to Georgia in America. The most recent *Homo erectus* fossils from Africa, dating from about a million years ago, indicate an evolution towards *Homo sapiens*.

A shift to bipedal locomotion may not be all that difficult for a primate. The change from chimpanzee to

Australopithecus is considered a smaller step than that from *Australopithecus* to *Homo*. Bipedalism was a crucial trait as the upright posture freed arms and hands for other roles, particularly for the making and using of tools. Ernst Mayr in *What Evolution Is* describes the shift from Australopithecine to *Homo* as the most profound in hominid history. The change resulted in the evolution of a series of characteristics: the brain size more than doubled, teeth became smaller, arms shortened, legs lengthened, and dimorphism—the physical difference between males and females of the same species—declined from a 50% to a 15% greater weight in males. The Australopithecines were threatened by other animals and had no weapons, such as horns or canines, with which to fend off the dangers. Some populations survived by using their wits to invent successful defense mechanisms, such as fire and rudimentary weapons. They were the first humans to make flaked stone tools, using the sharper flakes to construct spears. They used fires to protect themselves, warding off wild animals.

The point is: the descendants of the Australopithecines, who evolved into *Homo*, survived and prospered. The integrated patterns of behavior required for planning and fashioning tools were accomplished at least 2.5 million years ago. An advanced code for vocal communication may have existed. Records show the first recognizable tools were produced in East Africa around this time. Humans this early had a propensity for culture, social relationships, and a sense of self-awareness.

A common misperception about the modern human is that we evolved in a kind of relay race, with one species existing at a time and developing from one form into the next. This is not the case. Many hominids evolved alongside each other, but only *Homo sapiens* survived. Scientists consider all people today to be members of this single species. *Homo sapiens* first began to appear 150 000 to 200 000 years ago, equipped with technologies similar to the early Neanderthals, who were the third last hominid species to exist alongside *Homo sapiens*. New finds revealed that *Homo floresiensis* (or Man of Flores) lived in isolation on the remote eastern Indonesian island of Flores as recently as 13 000 years ago. *Homo floresiensis*, who rarely stood over a meter, is, for obvious reasons, nicknamed the hobbit.

Longstanding arguments exist in the scientific community regarding the emergence of modern humans from Africa and spreading throughout the world. The Centre of Origin postulates that a later *Homo sapiens*, known as Cro-Magnons, spread from Africa to the rest of the world 50 000 years ago. Around 35 000 years ago, a wave of *Homo sapiens* reached Western Europe, and after thousands of years of coexistence, the Neanderthal disappeared. The cause of their disappearance is still debated, but it is thought the extinction was the direct result of the Cro-Magnon migrating to Europe. No Neanderthal remains older than 28 000 years have surfaced. *Homo sapiens* and the Neanderthal clearly were contemporaries.

The question of whether *Homo sapiens* and Neanderthals interbred has not been answered. Despite genetic traces of Neanderthal in modern humans, theoretically, distinct species should be unable to interbreed. Modern humans generally have skeletons that are more delicate and DNA comparisons show that Cro-Magnons differed widely from the Neanderthals. Yet, skeletal remains of a child with robust body proportions found at the

Abrigo do Lagar Velho rock shelter in Portugal's Lapedo Valley do suggest the possibility of interbreeding.

The three areas distinguishing humans from other mammals are size of brain and the ability to use fire and language. Evidence of fire use was found in Kenya dating back 1.5 million years, but burnt soil could have been the result of lightning strikes, as there is no evidence of cooking or habitual fire use at this time. Evidence of controlled fires was found in Hula Valley, Israel, dating from 800 000 years. There is convincing evidence of fire 400 000 years ago in Europe at the French site, Terra Amata. Here, fire hearths, along with charred animal bones, were found. Nevertheless, abundant evidence of fire use only exists from 100 000 years ago. The ability to use fire would have given *Homo sapiens* a distinct advantage over other peoples in providing protection from cold and deterring predators. Cooking would have provided digestible food and parasite-free meat. Fire has also long served as a focal point for social congress.

The increase in brain size accelerated when the Australopithecine's environment was threatened, giving rise to upright bodies and bipedalism. *Homo rudolfensis* and *H. erectus* were the earliest recorded species at this level of hominization. *Homo rudolfensis* had a brain size of 700-900 cc.—double that of the Australopithecus brain, which averaged 450 cc. Growth in brain size slowed after *H. rudolfensis*, followed by a rapid increase in *H. erectus* 600 000 years back, when size further increased to 800–1 000 cc. The tendency continued for 500 000 years, when brain growth tapered off at 1 350 cc. although the Neanderthal brain attained 1 600 cc., due probably to their robust build. From then on, as if brain size no longer gave advantage, the greatest contribution to survival was intelligence. Brain capacity is now the distinguishing factor setting humans apart from other species. Despite the transition from hunter-gatherers to city civilizations, and advances in agriculture and technology, there has been no further increase in brain size. The rapid development of the brain is likely the result of speech and communication, which, once accomplished, required no larger brain.

The larger brain size complicated the process of giving birth. Records show that an increase in the size of the birth canal was incompatible with the upright posture of bipedalism. Brain growth now had to occur after birth, as infants needed to be born before the head grew too large. The mother's arms were no longer used for climbing, but engaged in the care of infants. At birth, newborns could be said to be seventeen months premature if compared to the maturity of quadrupeds at birth. The brain of the human baby almost doubles in size in its first year. This ingenious evolutionary change allows the size of the birth canal to remain the same. This adaptation has its drawbacks, since the infant is dependent on its parents for a much longer period.

The complex brain means that offspring need to learn from their parents and social group, until adequately equipped to interact with the environment on their own. Only in species with long term parental care is information handed down from generation to generation without it being carried in the genetic code. Information transferred from animal parent to offspring is limited, whereas humans develop throughout life. The transfer of cultural information in humans is a major influence on our development, bringing with it the sophisticated communication of spoken and written language.

Communication in animals is about giving and receiving signals. After fifty years of coaching, chimpanzees show little ability to use language with syntax. The development of speech stimulates and enlarges the brain. The areas processing information, storage, and memory are particularly well developed in humans.

The larger human brain led to arts, culture, literature, mathematics, and science. It is also responsible for consciousness and conscience. Humans can choose at will and have developed the spiritual awareness through which they postulate the soul. Humans are so far ahead that if evolution were to run its course, it would take millions of years for any other species to catch up. Language and the subsequent notion of an afterlife give us a head start in the evolutionary stakes.

An early form of symbolic thinking originates in South Africa at Blombos Cave. Snail shells, gathered from an estuary and pierced with a bone awl, possibly to string together as a necklace or bracelet, date 75 000 years ago. Some of the beads and tools are engraved and painted with red ochre —an indication of premeditated behavior. Similar examples of symbolic thinking from a similar time have been found in Botswana, Kenya, Ethiopia, Tanzania, and Israel.

It is commonly accepted that the Cro-Magnons were the first to engage in burial rituals, displaying signs of a belief in an afterlife. Ian Tattersall, curator of physical anthropology at the American Museum of Natural History in New York, explains how the Cro-Magnons were already creating art on the walls of caves 30 000 years ago. Clay was modelled occasionally, which may have had a magical or religious function. Bodies were decorated and buried with artefacts, which points to belief in an afterlife. Tattersall explains how the lives of the Cro-Magnons were entwined with symbolism. No other early humans left such a telling record. At a site in Sungir, Russia, two young individuals and a sixty-year-old male were buried with material riches.

The opulence of Cro-Magnon burial culture hints at social strata and labor division. Some bodies were flexed and others stretched out. Some graves were covered with rock slabs. Artefacts vary from place to place, reflecting cultural diversity. Prior to the Cro-Magnons, it seems that innovation was rare. Early art and symbolism elsewhere paled by comparison. They eventually abandoned their nomadic hunter-gatherer existence to settle in villages, some of which expanded into towns and cities. These early farmers cultivated wheat, rye, peas, lentils, and other plants and raised domesticated animals, such as cattle, sheep, pigs, and goats. They made pottery vessels for cooking and storing food, fashioned sickles out of stone for harvesting crops, and used flat stones as querns for grinding grain into flour. Though revolutionary, these changes took place gradually, over thousands of years.

The practice of ritualistic burial and belief in an afterlife evolved over time. Humans did not start burying their dead all of a sudden 6 000 years ago when, according to *Genesis*, the Creator endowed Adam with a soul. Rituals to accompany souls into the spirit world developed over at least 70 000 years. Did ritual burial arise out of mere superstition? Or is it that humans were evolving spiritually and were beginning to recognize, in addition to their evolving body and mind, the beginnings of a further dimension to their being: the soul?

Chapter 9

Ego / I

Today, many accept the soul as an integral aspect of their being. Yet, the inception thereof has never been an evolutionary step. A spiritual consciousness among humans already existed prior to the establishment of Mesopotamian civilization with its temples, houses, and burial chambers. Christianity, citing the Bible as reference, assumes that Adam was the first man and the first to receive a God-given soul. Other religions were also well established around 7 000 years ago, a millennium before Adam. The biblical story only rings true if one assumes that all other humans before Adam were soulless creatures.

Customarily, angels link the Creator with humans. Ancient texts, such as the Bible, record various incidents of angels appearing to humans to give them messages from God. Ascribed to angels is their ability to transcend space and time. They enter and exit the physical realm and alternative realities at will and reside in the realm of God. In the Old Testament, life on Earth took a quantum leap when Adam became a living soul, distinguishing him from the rest of the animal kingdom and humanity. But how, if indeed possible, would angels manage such a feat? Likely, it is nothing but myth. But the idea of a spiritual creature being part of a spiritual realm and taking on human form still applies. Why would these developing civilizations speculate about something as bizarre as angels and souls? Could it be that a new kind of human—through evolution—started making its appearance: one with a spiritual nature such as the soul? My name for such a soul-empowered being is *Homo angelicansis*.

Evolution is a change in the gene pool of a population over time. Hereditary genes pass from one generation to the next. The instructions for life are in the sequence of the DNA. Through procreation and reproduction, mutations in the genetic material cause change, and it is this process of change that we call evolution. Individual organisms cannot evolve, since they retain the same genetic material throughout a lifetime. Enough mutations in a branch of a species give rise to a new species. The entire species does not need to mutate in unison for a new species to evolve. It is characteristic of evolution that only the fittest survive. Organisms that rise to the challenge and adapt to environmental change are the ones that make it. If the soul is essential for the survival of a species, then those with soul and their offspring should flourish.

Should the *entire* species change over time, it remains the same species only more evolved. Even if the species changes dramatically, it remains the same species. However, if mutations take place in a sector of a larger group of the same species, that strain can develop differently enough to spawn a new species. The gradual process of evolution allows a sub-species to evolve and exist alongside its master-species, without it being apparent that the secondary species already exists. Initially, the changes are small and barely recognizable.

Directive evolution—the altering of genes by human manipulation—means that other species are at the mercy of the dominant species. It could also happen that the dominant within a species are not necessarily the fittest. Nonetheless, this very act signals the end of evolution and survival of the fittest. Humans have now advanced to a point where they can re-engineer biological organisms. With intellect and technology, they can override and redirect evolutionary processes, heralding the end of natural selection. This could be a blessing, but it also spells danger. Interference in the natural process does not ensure improvement, for remodeling can only take place on a biological level. It seems that we may be underestimating the awesome intelligence of evolution. We do not know everything about the nature of life, so it follows that we cannot determine how to create the fittest. Presently, the focus is on vanity. Creating generations fit enough to space migrate is another, but this seems only to entertain the select few involved in science.

The transplantation of organs in humans to sustain and prolong life is revolutionary enough, but hardly comparable with genetic manipulation through biotechnology, which alters the makeup of a cell and even transfers genes within and across species for improved or even new organisms. What are we trying to do? Create super humans? Space cadets? Immortality? We know that athletes use performance enhancing drugs to win competitions—with the knowledge and help of their governments. Why not genetic manipulation as well?

Speeding up change in this way, to supersede the pace of evolution, poses serious ethical questions. Death advances evolution. Prolonging life indefinitely may negate the attraction of an afterlife. Evolution thrives by way of genetic mutations through the process of allele appearing in the offspring of new generations. The artificial prolongation of life reintroduces *elderly* genes retrogressively affecting evolution.

I wonder if evolution applies to the soul. If all life springs from evolution, perhaps there are genes—material or spiritual—that give rise to the soul? Dr. Dean H Hamer, discoverer of the controversial *gay gene*, argues that some spirituality is coded into genes. Known as the God gene, VMAT2 is a part of the human genome. People with the God gene show signs of being self-transcendent, making spirituality a human inheritance and little more than an instinct.

In October 1990, the Human Genome Project (HGP) gained an understanding of the approximately 30 000 genes constituting the human blueprint. Coordinated by the US Department of Energy and the National Institute of Health, the international effort was carried out by numerous research companies. At the cost of billions of dollars and lasting more than a decade, one of the goals was to sequence the three billion DNA subunits. The genome provides unparalleled understanding of genes and chromosomes. Genes are identified in the nucleus of a cell and their location is pinpointed on the chromosomes in the nucleus. Our understanding of the genetic blueprint is, thus far, limited to linkage mapping and physical mapping.

Linkage mapping identifies the order of genetic landmarks along a chromosome where each marker has a unique DNA sequence. Physical mapping is a more precise method of placing genes or landmark sequences at specific distances from one another on a chromosome. The human genome sequence enables us to understand and combat human disease with new cures. Yet, despite a greater understanding of human biology and individuality, these advances cast no light on a spiritual nature.

In summary, there are three hypotheses regarding the origins and nature of spirituality: the soul being the product of God breathing soul into Adam; the soul arising from a spiritual realm, incarnating via humans, gaining Earthly experience and enlightenment; and now the soul genetically evolving from one generation to the next.

Chapter 10

Heaven

The idea of a hidden heaven is common to all religions. Gods and spiritual entities dwell in heaven and the soul is accepted therein after death. Ancient civilizations saw heaven as a physical place. Others believed it resides in the dark areas of the night sky. Christianity teaches that the pinnacle of spiritual achievement is the metamorphosis of an Earthly being into one with a resurrected body, which will be accepted into heaven. In the *Book of Revelation*s, John is shown by God how heaven is built of gold and glass in twelve layers, each inlaid with a different precious gem. In modern times, however, the idea of a physical heaven has been replaced with a yet undiscovered dimension.

The Holy Roman Catholic Church proposes purgatory, an intermediate destination, which precedes entry to heaven. It is a kind of correctional facility, where some souls go for purification. The doctrine holds that all who enter purgatory will eventually reach heaven. Purgatory between death and heaven is most likely a fabrication to cover the biblical time lapse. Since not all Christians die at the same time, a time of lingering from death to judgement day was required. Yet, even the Vatican has its doubts about limbo. In 2006, BBC news reported how the Vatican was to review the state of limbo and stated that Pope Benedict was considering an amendment to its doctrine. The reason being that the theory had originated during the Middle Ages as a solution to the knotty theological question over the souls of babies who died too young to have committed any sin. The Vatican is worried about people in developing countries turning to Islam, whose doctrine makes the souls of stillborn babies go straight to paradise. Purgatory has no scriptural basis, however. The first mention of purgatory comes from the letter of Nicholas of Saint Albans of 1176 AD, which was ratified by Rome in 1254.

Charismatic Christianity follows St. Paul, who taught that acknowledgement that Jesus is Lord and faith that God raised Him from the dead are the exclusive requirements for salvation (*Romans 10:8-10*). James, Jesus's half-brother, asserts that man is justified by faith and works. (*James 2:24 & 26*). The Catholic establishment makes entry into heaven conditional upon Christians receiving God's grace by way of the sacraments of baptism, the Eucharist, and confession. The perfect life with God in heaven is to reside in a state of supreme happiness. For Protestants, entry into heaven depends upon one's faith in Jesus and is predetermined by the grace of God, with all Christians having been chosen for redemption since the beginning of time. The Armenians teach that faith in Christ, through an act of free will, is the way to redemption, while Universalism thinks all will eventually be saved, regardless of religious belief.

The eastern equivalent of purgatory is Pure Land. With an emphasis on reincarnation, one stream of Buddhism is based upon the Pure Land Sutras or Western Paradise Sutras. Having originated in India around the turn of the first century AD, the doctrine spread to China, becoming popular in the fourth century. Pure Land is central to the precepts inspired by Amitabha Buddha, a monk instructed by the eighty-first Buddha, Lokesvararaja. Pure Land sees no need for meditation or ritual. The only requirement for rebirth is the spoken repetition of the phrase *Homage to the Buddha Amitabha*, who promised a far more lavish Buddha land to his followers than did his predecessors.

The doctrine of Pure Land spread to Japan, reaching prominence in the twelfth century when monk Honen Shonin established the sect, Jodo Shinshu or Shin. Honen also preached perpetual elicitation of Amida through dance and chant. Shin became popular for its simplicity in veneration. Pure Land Buddhism is a branch of mainstream Mahayana Buddhism, in which fortunate souls reincarnate prior to their final attainment of Nirvana—the Buddhist equivalent of heaven. To attain Nirvana, union with the cosmos is required and human desire extinguished; this perfection of the soul is achieved through successive transmigrations. Since Nirvana is virtually unattainable from earthly life, Pure Land is the intermediary phase, before reaching the ultimate destination. Nirvana, which is impossible to define and can only be realized through individual experience, differs from heaven in that it is not a place and can therefore be reached without dying. Nirvana, derived from the Sanskrit, means *extinguishing*, implying a *blowing out* of a fire or candle flame. In Nirvana, the flames of desire, lust, hatred, greed, suffering, and ignorance are extinguished through endless cycles of transmigration. Through sequential cycles of reincarnation, humans can perfect the soul. In the Buddhist context, the person realizing Nirvana is compared to a fire extinguished when its fuel is finished.

The belief of a benevolent god residing in heaven is usually contrasted with the antonym of a devil in hell. For the Babylonians, hell was located within the planetary spheres, a place of no return. In Greek and Roman mythology, Hades and Tartarus were situated in the underworld. Entrance into heaven was conditional, so that those not meeting the criteria were banished to this place of eternal punishment. Zoroaster, at the turn of the sixth century, shaped most of the sinister imagery of hell: a dark underground place laden with fires and molten rock where unbelievers were tormented. The Devil or Satan was depicted as a red creature with horns, a pitchfork, and a long tail with a diamond shaped end.

In occultism, heaven is known as *devachan*. Several deaths occur before the attainment of *devachan*. The first is when the body dies. Subsequently, there is a gradual disintegration of the lower principles or quaternary of man in *kamaloka* (occult version of purgatory). The second death occurs when the etheric body dissolves during *kamaloka*, three or four days after the death of the physical body. The third death happens years after *kamaloka*, when the astral body dies, allowing the higher ternary of man to be separated from the lower quaternary and freed for the ultimate destination of *devachan*, where previous incarnations are realized at a higher spiritual level. *Devachan* is the dwelling place of God and the nine celestial hierarchies of angelic beings. Deriving from the highest realm of God, the celestial hierarchies are hosts of beings capable of manifesting in the physical realm of Earth.

There is much speculation about a heavenly paradise awaiting us. When the body dies, so do the mind and personality. The soul disappears too, lost forever from the Earth realm. All that lingers is the spirit of the person in our memories. We do not find the soul in the observable universe; if it survives, it must be elsewhere. But where in the fabric of our universe can the soul exist? In what dimension or vibration will one find the soul? Why does the soul appear to have mystical powers akin to that of angelic beings, seemingly existing outside the observable reality?

Chapter 11

The Soul

In the world of science, organic matter with the anatomy of a living organism has no maker. Science does not acknowledge esoteric life-giving principles such as prana, chi, or spirit. Neither does it recognize etheric and astral realms as supportive realities to the material nature. Science does not consider the sequential unfolding of evolutionary events as premeditated, directed, or choreographed by a higher being. Science cannot acknowledge a force it cannot measure or a god it cannot find. Organisms originated spontaneously and reproduction occurs spontaneously. The inability to understand the animation of matter leads scientists to discard the notion that a supernatural force is running the evolutionary universe. How, then, can two near identical cells exist side by side, one alive, the other without life? What differentiates dead matter from living matter?

Evolutionary science determines that all life results from a single moment when matter formed a structure with a potential for life. Initially, the way atoms organized to form a physio-chemical structure with life happened by chance. Similar structures managed to stay alive long enough to pass their blueprints onto offspring. The repeated change and improvement caused a sustained animation. What causes living atoms to group and form a living structure is not clear, but, for science, a life-bestowing principle such as spirit does not exist.

Steven Rose, professor of biology, justifies how the spontaneous formation of life may have started nearly four billion years ago, evolving to its current status. Drawing from a variety of sources, Rose explains how everything originated with chemistry. Life, however defined, engages the interactions and interconversions of chemicals built from carbon, hydrogen, oxygen, and nitrogen. These molecules float in a watery sea with ions of sodium, potassium, calcium, chlorine, sulfur, phosphorus, and a range of heavy metals. Initially, the inorganic chemistry of the cooling earth changed into the organic carbon chemistry of sugars, amino acids, and nucleotides, which in turn became the building blocks of nucleic acids. From then on, the giant molecules such as proteins, fats, DNA, and RNA developed, incorporating phosphorus, sulfur, and the rest along the way. This could have happened in several ways, the simplest being synthesis in places such as oceans, volcanic eruptions, or possibly clay areas where land and water mingle. Life may even have resulted from activity in outer space, where fierce electrical storms set the initial process in motion. Abiotic synthesis theories like these are not exclusive, and whether one or all scenarios were in play, the result was that organic chemicals covered the oceans and its margins.

Jumping from a lifeless patch of chemicals to the emerging life is a huge leap. The answer may lie in the lipids of the ocean. Oil on the surface of water either spreads as a thin film or forms droplets. These droplets have a property that concentrates the organic chemicals within them. A lipid membrane creates an inside and an outside—the basis for the environment of any potential organism. The droplet becomes a proto-cell, with an internal chemical constitution different from that on its outside. This separation is the primary characteristic of any living organism. The difference between the inside and outside indicates a potential for self and non-self. Computer models show how mutually interacting chemicals stabilize to form a dynamic metabolic web. Larger organic molecules can form within this type of web. Eventually strings of amino acids or nucleic acids (RNA) catalyze their own synthesis, enabling acceleration and further syntheses.

The ionic composition inside the proto-cell involves catalytic processes whereby the internal concentration of the ions becomes different to that outside the cell. A simple lipid membrane will not achieve specificity, for it cannot readily select what may enter and what it must exclude. In living cells, however, the semi-permeable membrane is selective and chooses ions or molecules that may enter or leave. Somehow, a variety of proteins in the lipid environment must have been incorporated into the lipid proto-cell membrane at a relatively early stage. This configuration for life potential is fundamental to the start of a living organism. The difference in voltage on the inside and the outside of living cells and membranes can be measured. Two electrodes, one inside the membrane of a modern living cell and another on the external surface connected to a voltmeter, will record a significant voltage difference between the inside and the outside of the cell. The inside of the cell is negative and the outside positive. This membrane potential is as defining as any other aspect of cell structure and biochemistry. All proto-cells need energy for internal stability and survival. They also require energy to grow and divide. The oceanic environment has sufficient energy in the form of synthesized molecules, such as sugars. Eventually, these proto-cells acquired the capacity to capture energy from the sun, tapping the atmospheric supply of carbon dioxide. Using solar energy to synthesize sugars through photosynthesis, organisms generated and released oxygen. Billions of years later, the Earth has an oxygen-rich and carbon-dioxide-poor atmosphere.

Faithful reproduction was the next significant evolutionary step. Drawing in ever more material, proto-cells grew to a stage of losing stability, and split in two. Primitive reproduction does not yet represent faithful reproduction or replication. For similar offspring cells, the same pattern of proteins must be present in each. Here is where the mechanism for faithful reproduction starts to play a role. Accurate synthesis of complex molecules, where each daughter cell is identical, requires RNA and DNA. The former exists as a single strand molecule, while in DNA two strands are entwined to form a double helix. DNA strands can separate, forming a template for another strand. But there is still uncertainty whether early replication is based on RNA or DNA. Rose notes a paradox in this regard: enzymes and energy are required to synthesize a nucleic acid molecule from scratch, and controlled energy production requires enzymes and cellular mechanisms. If proto-cells are to turn into fully-fledged cellular organisms, there must have been some bootstrapping: a self-help situation whereby the molecules in cellular energy trading are chemically related to the molecular building blocks from which the nucleic acids are assembled. This view is unresolved but based on well informed speculation.

Cells with higher efficiency for capturing and using energy and replicating more faithfully have a greater chance of survival than do less efficient cells. Two evolutionary processes happen simultaneously: competition, where rivals struggle for survival, or co-operation, where cells work together. At this point, one of the most important stages—a defining feature of life where cells can metabolize and replicate—is in place. From here, symbiosis and competition also occur. The presence of a semi-permeable boundary separating self from non-self gives the potential for metabolism to self-repair and maintain itself. Finally, the potential for reproduction of faithful copies of the self is in place. These features require adaptability: the capacity to respond to and act upon the environment to enhance survival and replication. It is this behavior principle that Rose categorizes as life. At its simplest, behavior does not require brains or a nervous system. What it does require is something like a program. The program must be flexible in adapting to short- and long-term challenges from the external environment. For long term survival, this must be sustained until replication is achieved.

Somewhere in evolutionary history, cells grouped into larger aggregates. The propensity for cells to group and find mutual benefit is profound. The merit of social living is that individual cells no longer respond adaptively to rapid changes in its environment. The survival of an individual cell becomes dependent on the survival of the organism. In a multi-cellular setup, co-operation is through communication. Cells specialize through an action known as homeostasis where stability is achieved through dynamics not stasis. The needs of individual cells are subordinated and behavior becomes a property of the organism.

A nervous system evolved to meet the need for a direct line of communication through which messages are conveyed electrically or chemically. With increasingly complex forms of behavior, specialized cells evolved. Multicellular organisms evolved brains with the capacity for cognition. The brain evolved, eventually making humans the smartest animals on Earth. Complex multi-cellular organisms, such as ourselves, continue to be concerned with survival; better strategies and differential reproduction improve the chance of survival. Developing brains imposed co-operation and competition, and although brains develop cognitive skills, cognition must have a purpose.

The purpose of cognition is surpassed by emotion—animals learn and remember for a purpose, which includes effect. Information is empty without a system to interpret it and give it meaning. Animals with brains secrete hormones that interact with their brains. Learning involves emotions, which engage more powerfully than the brain. *Homo sapiens* currently surpasses all species. Their uniqueness lies in versatility. Humans are outclassed in virtually every other department by other animals, but they are the pentathlon experts. Humans have developed language, consciousness, and foresight, along with sophisticated structures of society, culture, and technology. They are also the only animals capable of describing or writing about their achievements. And, as far as we know, we are the only animals to express a concept of the supernatural.

The belief in a creator upholding life through the vital principle of spirit has been around for some time. Assuming for a moment there is a life-giving force, if the original structure was infused with life, but subsequently died, it would have meant the end of the entire cycle of life. The premature death of the first cell would have put an end to the potentiality of continued life and evolution. By replicating itself, however, the first successful organism passed its life onto the next. And life continued. Organisms with life have no sway over this life-giving ability. To stay alive, they must maintain material form. And even though change takes place through growth and aging, the material composition of the organism cannot change significantly without losing its life principle. Life remains with each organism for a period, then ceases to exist, but if the Life principle is passed from organism to organism, continued existence is assured.

Life in matter only had to succeed once and then replicate the achievement. To sustain life, replication must succeed without fail. If there is ever a break in the process, life would cease to exist; there is no guarantee of successful repetition. Not only must an organism behave as if imbued with an informant, but its sub-components, right down to the cells, atoms, and sub-particles, must collectively behave as if alive. Imagine the magnitude of particles required to fall into place, behaving in unity, to form the anatomy of one cell. Yet science has decreed that there is no informant causing this animation. There is no life-giving principle transforming a chemical structure into a biological one—the ghost in the machine—appearing to imbue it with spirit.

Even so, neither life-giving force nor life-giving spirit is the soul! The soul is not the giver of life, for it also seeks life. For billions of years, organisms had life but no soul. The soul, if it exists, came later.

One of the biggest questions regarding the soul is whether it is an evolutionary trait. Having shown how complex life came about, could the soul be integral to that process? Once the material body dies, does the soul require a life-giving force called the spirit? The question of whether the soul is independent of the life force or part of evolution is crucial, for it could be the crowning glory of natural selection. The soul, however, has not made the evolutionary journey from the beginning and is not the giver of life, for it too seeks life to sustain its animation. Seen in this light, the *evolutionary* role of the soul becomes apparent.

Chapter 12

Space-time

The study of space has fascinated scientists for thousands of years. In its earliest form, geometers from ancient Egypt, Sumer, and Babylonia calculated right angles for the corners of buildings. They found that all measurements are only possible in three directions perpendicular to each other. For these early scientists, the three dimensions of space were absolutes. Initially, time had little to do with calculating space, but that changed when Zeno, the fifth century BC Greek mathematician, described paradoxes relating to space.

Devising a canny mind experiment, Zeno showed the impossibility of a runner reaching a winning post. From a mathematical perspective, the distance would have to be covered at half the distance at a time. The problem arises when the distance is halved ad infinitum. Covering half the distance an infinite number of times would take forever. The runner would get closer to the finish line, without ever reaching the destination. This is not true of life, as a runner does reach the finish line. Similarly, the time it takes to cover a minimum distance is negligible. Space and time cannot regress by infinitely small degrees, because eventually they reach an indivisible minimum. This demonstrates that the concept of space, time, and motion is not straightforward. In physics, the line cannot be merely the sum of points and time is not merely fractions of a specific period. To cross the finish line, both space and time would need a minimum. The true natures of space and time are unclear: either they are continuous or can be divided in half ad infinitum.

Max Planck, the German physicist and father of quantum theory, calculated the smallest measurement of length that has meaning as 10^{-33} centimeters. Known as the Planck length, this quantum is too minute to detect. Since the beginning of the twentieth century, the Planck length has formed the basis of quantum mechanics. Planck also invented the smallest unit of meaningful time as 10^{-43} of a second. Planck time is calculated by the time it takes light to travel the distance of a Planck length. Planck length and time helps make sense of objects such as the line and plane as composed of zero-dimensional points. Attempting to reduce space and time more finely becomes meaningless. Nobody knows what happens at this scale and beyond. Space and time at such infinitesimal measurements call for new rules—such as extra dimensions.

Physicists around 500 BC speculated that space was flat, in which case travelling far enough in a straight line would result in falling off the edge of the Earth to join the stars or the dark regions in space. Around this time, Greek philosophers studying ships appearing on the horizon realized that the Earth could not be flat. If it were, the ship would start small and increase in size as it travelled closer. But ship's sails first appear on the horizon, followed by rest of the ship, as if rising from the sea.

Third century BC mathematician, Euclid, largely responsible for the principles of geometry and mathematics, defined the universe in three dimensions of space. Space of this nature is consistent with everyday experience and ordinary measurement of size and distance. Euclid's fifth postulate showed it is only possible to draw one line parallel to another through a point next to the initial line. This, baffled physicists for more than 2 000 years, and it is only in the nineteenth century that answers emerged. Since Euclid dealt with flat surfaces, the mathematics of the fifth postulate requires that space must be straight or flat—any line in or through the universe would remain infinitely straight.

Nineteenth century mathematicians explored the idea of space being curved. Karl Friedrich Gauss, Nikolai Lobachevsky, and Janos Bolyai independently discredited Euclid's fifth postulate of the unique parallel. To demonstrate how a consistent geometric system in which Euclid's fifth postulate is replaced by a new one, they introduced abstract mathematical constructs known as non-Euclidean geometry. Parallel lines can cross one another—if space is curved. A familiar example are the lines of latitude on the surface of the Earth, which start parallel at the equator, yet cross at the poles. The German mathematician Bernhard Riemann then developed the mathematical framework that demonstrated the curved nature of space. With the weight of a body causing space to warp around it, it would mean that the entire universe consists of warped spaces.

In the late nineteenth century, British physicist James Clerk Maxwell discovered that electricity and magnetism are closely related in the form of electromagnetic waves. The concept of travelling through space at the speed of light led to the conclusion that light was a wave and that it must move in a medium called ether. In 1887, Albert Michelson and Edward Morley, in one of the most significant tests ever performed, were unable to isolate ether, thereby disproving the theory. To this day, ether remains undetectable or non-existent. At that point, time had had little to do with measuring space, but this was about to change.

At the beginning of the twentieth century, our perception of space changed when the German-born physicist, Albert Einstein, discovered how the three dimensions of space are intrinsically linked with time. Solving some of the most perplexing scientific problems of our time, Einstein, between 1905 and 1915, came forth with a special theory of relativity and a general theory of relativity. Building on Maxwell's idea that all observers experience the speed of light in the same way, Einstein showed how space should not be conceived as three-dimensional, but is linked with time in such a way that it forms a four-dimensional space-time continuum.

In a stroke of brilliance, Einstein showed how the fourth dimension is not a spatial component, but one of duration. In special relativity, there is no preferred state of rest in space—are all relative. Thus, observers with differing motion will—despite experiencing the speed of light the same—experience simultaneous events differently. At different velocities, events differ in time. The relative experience of space-time is not an illusion, but a real phenomenon. In daily life, time and space are experienced as absolutes due to relative slow motion. Approaching the speed of light, however, speed becomes absolute and space-time relative. In four-dimensional space-time, time stands still for anything travelling at the speed of light. Photons travelling at light speed experience no time. This explains why photons still carry information of the big bang nearly fourteen billion years after the event.

With general relativity, the structure of special theory is adapted to include gravity. In general relativity, Einstein found that even gravity, the weakest of the four known forces, will affect the way space-time behaves. As much as time is intrinsic and inseparable to space, space-time is intrinsically linked to the distribution of matter. The curvature caused by gravity extends to four-dimensional space-time. By adopting Riemann's geometry, Einstein could predict how gravity indeed curves space and time.

In general relativity, the effect of gravitation close to mass deforms space-time around it. The degree of curvature depends on the mass of the object. The relationship between space, time, and matter is relative—again depending on the state of motion of the observer. The entire universe is dynamic, with varying measures of space-time. It is impossible to distinguish between being pulled by the gravity of a planet and being accelerated by a lift. A line is no longer straight, but the shortest distance between two points—and it does not have to be straight.

Einstein's brilliance set the stage for space travel. Half a century after his discoveries, man landed on the moon. Another forty years later, a craft landed on Mars. In 2017, exactly a century after Einstein published General

Relativity, US President Donald Trump signed legislation approving human exploration of Mars, setting NASA's intention to land people on the red planet by the mid-2030s.

Einstein's introduction of time as the fourth dimension is arguably the most significant discovery of all time. However, it is also one of the biggest distractions, for setting in motion the era of space-flight brought an end to the search for the fourth dimension of space. It also set in stone the notion of there being no heaven out there. For nearly a century, the focus has shifted to colonizing the universe in spaceships and spacesuits. However, as we will see next, space had yet another ace up its sleeve and was soon to reveal one of its darkest secrets.

Chapter 13

Hyperspace

In 1922, American astronomer Edwin Hubble demonstrated that some of the starlit spots in the night sky are galaxies; the Milky Way galaxy is but one of billions scattered throughout the universe. In 1929, he discovered that galaxies are flying apart from each other and that the universe is expanding. Further contributions regarding extra dimensions came from Polish mathematician Theodor Kaluza and Swedish mathematician Oskar Klein, who independently proposed an unseen fourth spatial dimension. With the help of Einstein's theory of relativity, they set out to unify the forces of gravity and electromagnetism, which seemed more readily explained in five-dimensional space-time. Although the experiment failed, the introduction of an extra spatial dimension is relevant to the study of spirituality.

An expanding universe raises the question of repercussions when expansion runs out of steam. With energy density overtaking critical density, the universe, in time, should stop expanding and collapse under the influence of gravity. Discovering whether gravity would ultimately halt expansion and pull matter back into a big crunch had cosmologists calculating the mass in the universe. To their surprise, the amount of visible and detectable matter in the universe does not add up! The distribution of visible matter for an expanding universe turns out to be far less than the critical, suggesting there must be some form of undetected dark matter. The visible matter of the universe makes up five percent of the critical value. Ninety-five percent of matter is either missing or undetectable. Matter of this nature seems to consist of non-luminous material, undetectable with telescopes or electromagnetic radiation. Currently, the presence of dark matter is deduced from the motions of solar systems, galaxies, and superclusters.

Studying supernova (exploding stars), astronomers in 1998 noticed the expansion rate of the universe is accelerating. Observing the redshift (spectral differences toward longer wavelengths), they found that supernovae further away from Earth are moving faster when compared to those closer. With galaxies further away receding faster than their neighbors, the rate of expansion must be increasing. Apparently, dark matter is not enough to explain this expansion. If anything, there must be dark energy. In opposition to the attractive nature of gravity, dark energy must repel ordinary matter, causing expansion to accelerate. Subsequent measurements indicate that the universe is composed of one-third dark matter and two-thirds dark energy.

The idea of dark energy has long been postulated. In 1917, Einstein proposed a constant form of energy represented by the cosmological term *Lambda*. Assuming the universe is static, he was unable to construct a universe with only matter and curvature. Continual gravitational attraction of matter would cause the universe eventually to collapse in upon itself. To counterbalance the attractive gravitational force, he introduced an ad hoc cosmological constant. But only twelve years later, Hubble discovered the universe was far from static; this discovery forced Einstein to abandon Lambda. His apparent mistake, which Einstein considered the biggest blunder of his career, had to wait out the century before receiving recognition when the cosmological constant was resurrected with the predication of dark energy.

The quest for dark matter and dark energy makes for one of the most exciting challenges in modern science. Some argue dark matter may consist of exotic elementary particles different from known matter. Minute particles and larger structures for dark matter, such as neutrinos, brown dwarfs, and black holes, were proposed. Weakly Interacting Massive Particles (WIMPs) and white dwarfs also made their appearance. Not for the faint-hearted!

A unified theory of nature and the structure of the universe remains elusive. The problem lies in combining nature on a large scale with the sub-atomic level. Where general relativity provides a theoretical framework for understanding the universe on a large scale, quantum physics provides an understanding of subatomic particles. The two have yet to be conjoined to form an encompassing theory.

One of the most explored theories in physics is the Standard Model. As a physical theory, the Standard Model should explain how the elementary particles and fundamental forces of nature unite on a sub-atomic level. Since it only incorporates the electromagnetic, weak, and strong forces of particles, but not gravity, the Standard Model as a unifying theory is incomplete. Another limitation is its failure to explain the problem of the cosmological constant. The Standard Model also only explains the particles of the observable universe, excluding dark matter, which seemingly consists of particles yet to be discovered.

The unification of general relativity, quantum mechanics, and the unknown dark elements of nature remain elusive. The unification of the universe on both scales must explain all matter and all four of the known forces in nature on cosmic and quantum mechanical scales, and therefore requires a Standard Model, which includes gravity as well as the yet undetected dark matter and dark energy. This new physics is extremely challenging. Making matters ever more difficult is the impossibility of simultaneously specifying the position and momentum of a subatomic particle. Naming it the uncertainty principle, twentieth-century German physicist Werner Heisenberg showed how the action of measuring the position of a particle automatically causes a disturbance in its velocity as well.

Experiments to confirm extra dimensions are part of the mainstream physics of our day. String Theory, where particles and forces are described as tiny oscillating strings, is another theoretical framework that tries to marry quantum particles with gravity. Based on the Kaluza-Klein idea of extra dimensions, strings extend four-dimensional space-time to permeate a realm of ten, eleven, or perhaps as many as twenty-six dimensions. In String Theory, strings vibrate in at least ten space-time dimensions: four of Einstein's space-time plus six more curled up in the Planck length of 10^{-33} cm. String theory is still in the making and physicists are not sure of the outcome. The beauty of the theory lies in its anticipated ability to unify quantum and gravity. It also challenges the conventional idea that one cannot divide space and time smaller than the Planck length, while exploring the possibility that space-time has more than four dimensions. Since anything at this quantum would be too small to detect, some question whether this can stand as a valid theory.

Others have questioned that extra dimensions can only be as small as the Planck length. Theoretical physicists Lisa Randall and Raman Sundrum see an extra dimension stretching to infinity. Their work of 1999, RS-1 and RS-2, considers the universe evolving differently in the beginning and suggests the weakness of gravity points to a fifth dimension. Their papers explain why gravity could be a billion times weaker compared with electromagnetism and weak and strong nuclear forces.

Incorporating over ten thousand scientists and engineers from more than a hundred countries, the twenty-seven-kilometer circumference Large Hadron Collider (LHC) at CERN, near Geneva, makes for the most comprehensive and expensive experiment ever devised on Earth. The world's heftiest particle collider went into operation in 2010. Currently, the laboratory smashes energetic particles together, probing regions of space never observed before. Aiming to test the predictions of theories of particle physics, scientists try to measure the properties of the Higgs boson (coined the God particle) and search for particles predicted by supersymmetric theories, as well as attempting to resolve the interrelation between quantum mechanics and general relativity. Finally, if all goes to plan, they hope to discover the nature of dark matter and find evidence supporting extra dimensions. The impact of such discoveries would be profound.

Leaving Earth for greener pastures lies at the heart of space exploration. With Earth running out of real estate and resources, further exploitation will soon be impossible. Critical parameters in many parts are causing the extinction of species of fauna and flora threatened by the effects of global warming: the result of an over-abundance of carbon dioxide in the atmosphere—largely the consequence of the increasing human footprint. The survival of our Earth has become a real concern. For some time now, interplanetary, interstellar, and intergalactic migration have seemed the obvious solution. Easier said than done.

Distances between solar systems are so immense that hundreds of thousands of years would be required to reach the closest neighboring solar system, given the speed of current space travel. Relocating to anything farther than our own planetary system is implausible, and yet, some still insist that these journeys are possible. For author Thomas Georges, there are two paths to achieving this: replacing body parts and the brain or redesigning the organic body and mind from scratch. Eventually, the biological and mechanical paths will merge, making organic modifications, including new beings, possible. He does highlight the moral dilemma of playing God, saying there seems to be no limit to what we can do, so where does one stop? It is here that the distinction between extinction and immortality becomes blurry.

Armand Delsemme, retired professor of astrophysics at the University of Toledo in Ohio, sees genetic engineering as essential, irrespective of religious, moral, and ethical considerations. For him, the awakening of intelligence changed the rules of the game completely. Initially, he believes we will restrict ourselves to the correction of random genetic defects, but will later modify the human genome in directions yet unforeseen and with uncertain results. Ultimately, the reason for effecting such change is to ensure our long-term survival, which in turn will determine our ability to colonize the galaxy and beyond. Author John Gribbin thinks the answer lies in time travel. During the 1980s, theorists speculated about space-time travel via tunnels in space called wormholes. Another idea explored rotating cylinders, a type of time machine in space, capable of creating a drag on space-time.

Houston, we have a problem! Organic life cannot survive extended spaceflights in the harsh conditions of outer space. Jeffrey Sutton, a member of NASA's space medical research team, explains the vulnerability of bodies when subjected to even relatively short journeys in microgravity. In space, the body shows severe bone loss, at a rate of as much as 1 to 1.5% a month. Space travel therefore leads to an acceleration of age-related changes, like osteoporosis. Extended exposure to weightless environments also increases the risk of kidney stones and bone fractures. Astronauts experience loss of muscle mass, strength, and endurance. Microgravity affects the neurovestibular system, the integrated system of neural, sensory, and brain circuits that control balance, directional orientation, and stabilized vision. The body suffers blood volume loss, immunodeficiency, and transient post flight anemia or low red blood cell levels, even with optimum nutrition. Space radiation poses one of the greatest risks on prolonged missions, introducing cataracts and cancer and adversely affecting many physiological processes.

Making the body more durable, with a longer life span, will not get us very far in cosmic terms. Inter-stellar travel requires sustained life for hundreds of thousands of years. There is, of course, no technology, device, or resource to render such journeys possible. Even if we could prolong life long enough, evolution would become obsolete.

Gregory Stock, in *Redesigning Humans*, thinks we are on the cusp of profound change. For him, *Homo sapiens* is not the final word in primate evolution. Selection is not the key word either. With the help of genetics, humans will alter themselves. It is no longer a matter of if, but rather when, where, and how. Biological enhancement will challenge even the most basic ideas about what it means to be human. The modification of future generations will have unforeseen consequences. Once self-design starts, there is no telling where it will end, but it would transform evolution. With the propagation of successful genes, reproduction will become selective, faster, and more effective. Self-transformation will change future generations to be distinctly different from our contemporary species. A pseudo-extinction of this nature would result in the end of the lineage. Ultimately, disaster might strike, proving too complex to rework.

British astrophysicist Stephen Hawking, at a 2006 news conference in Hong Kong, suggested that humans could soon have a permanent base on Mars. For him, survival depends on finding new homes elsewhere in the universe. For Hawking, as with most scientists, space migration happens with the body intact. But is this the right option? With humanity being but a phase in the greater evolutionary unfolding of life, could there be another way of making such journeys possible? Astrophysicists Lawrence Krauss and Glenn Starkman raise the possibility of consciousness existing without the physical body and that humans will abandon their bodies altogether. Though futuristic, for them, shedding the body presents no fundamental difficulty. All it does is presume consciousness is not tied to a set of organic molecules, but can be embodied in a multitude of forms, from cyborgs to sentient interstellar clouds. Discarding the material form altogether does presents challenges.

Colonizing the universe with or without the material body intact are two differing approaches. Which one of the two will be successful? It depends where you want to go. Interstellar journeys will require more than light speed travel. To project mass nearly that fast requires infinite amounts of energy. More energy means more mass. It comes down to plausibility and affordability. The alternative is to divest the mass. If humanity cannot migrate with the material body intact, why not leave it behind? The massless body—that is, the soul—makes survival free from Earth a possibility. Might it be the key which unlocks the door to our future survival?

Chapter 14

Revelations

The time to rewrite the Book of Revelations has come.

With prophetic flourish, Apostle John, Saint of the Holy Roman Catholic Church, vividly describes the end times. His predictions may come true, but I do not think they will. Outcomes with more credibility regarding the fate of life on Earth may be derived from the disciplines of modern science and technology.

In composing this work, I have demonstrated the difficulty of proving the existence of a separable soul. It is by no means certain whether spirituality is real or imagined. Perhaps we are deluded. Nevertheless, by excluding the supernatural, there should be a way to examine spirituality from the scientific standpoint.

At the root of mind and consciousness is the evolving brain and its network of neurons. When the brain dies, the mind and its awareness also die. There is no evidence that mind and consciousness separate permanently from the material host. Nobody has returned from the finality of death to tell the tale. Not even near-death and out-of-body experiences verify a separation from the physiological structure. The way in which awareness flourishes poses the question whether it originates from another realm or extends there without the assistance of the brain, though with the help of a soul.

Where do we go from here? Does humanity persist with age-old tradition or has the game plan changed? Is the survival—the destiny—of Life on Earth dependent on the presence of a separable soul? If so, could it be that evolution must solve the problem of a soul on its own? Perhaps time will tell, but is there time for evolution to take its course? Or will humanity snatch the reins from Mother Nature's natural path, and in the process, prevent evolution from giving rise to the soul?

Evolution is a fundamental principle of nature that has, until now, remained free of interference. If the pace of evolution is lagging behind human progress, are those who assume the responsibility of establishing a future capable and ethical? Or, are they, with the help of genetic science, about to hamper man's chance of survival? Genetics in the hands of unscrupulous regimes, lacking the responsibility of foresight, could be a dangerous force.

As successful survivors, we have no apparent need for migration to other dimensions. Earth, for those who can afford it, is not such a bad place. But what if catastrophe threatens extinction? Would we think differently? All the wealth, pleasure, and play are worthless in the face of extinction. Yet, destruction looms as Earth faces catastrophe. Some such events are already appearing on the horizon; others will happen in the further future. It is worth pondering that—whatever the events—evolution triumphs, regardless of human interference.

Humanity is at a crossroads, where materialism may prevail over spirituality. But which course will ensure survival in the long term? The theory that matter is the only reality does not allow for a spiritual nature. Similarly, the idea of man originating from God and returning after passing could be mere fantasy. Continued evidence of the development of species through selection, however, gives credence to evolution. But does evolution have a spiritual component? To be precise, *Homo sapiens* is a material being with a body and a brain; the soul is not part of its classification. Acquiring an evolutionary soul means becoming a new kind of being: one with a spiritual body. A triune being with a soul constitutes a new species. I name this species *Homo angelicansis*.

Since its inception 3.8 billion years ago, Life has transformed the Earth. Life begins as a primitive force, evolving and changing as it populates the globe. Single-celled organisms develop into multicellular ones, culminating in complex beings with upright bodies and a brain. Life starts instinctively, but with the help of an ever-developing brain, it becomes intelligent, conscious, and then conscious of its consciousness. But Life remains restricted to the circumference of Earth. To occupy the biosphere, Life devises technology. Together with the understanding of four-dimensional space–time, Life takes to space travel. Yet, Life remains confined to a small region within its solar system. To spread its wings even further, Life unravels its blueprint—the genome. With godlike qualities, Life creates forms possessing greater robustness, making migration to other parts of its solar system possible. With omnipresence as a real potential, Life sets its sights on invading other solar systems, perhaps even the universe beyond. Occupying more than its own solar system, however, presents challenges. With vast distances making conventional space travel impossible, Life must expand its godlike capacity. Omnipotence needs a longer lifespan, preferably immortality, enabling Life to travel over longer periods of time and further into space. But, Life finds technology limiting. Even at near the speed of light, occupying the universe with a material body wrapped in a space suit and spaceship takes eons. To ensure occupation beyond its solar system, Life takes on a new form—the soul. And so, Life transcends physicality. Omnipotent, omnipresent, nonmaterial, and immortal, Life colonizes the universe and occupies alternative dimensions instead.

This description illustrates the role of humanity in Life's colonization of further habitats. Life does not favor a specific form. The human is but one of many expressions of Life. Many species have fallen by the wayside, unable to sustain living on Earth. Similarly, *Homo sapiens* will be replaced by beings more capable of sustaining Life beyond Earth. Inability to colonize the universe with the current form will cause Life to discard the human being. Initially, Life might favor a modified form modeled on *Homo sapiens*. A reconstructed human might be a dead end, though. Survival of the fittest implies the fitness of many aspects. Evolution provides endless variety in a way science cannot, relying as it does on the predetermined outcome of experiments.

Life is colonizing the universe; it is the mode of transport that needs resolution. Either Life migrates to alternative planetary systems in spaceships and spacesuits or it transmigrates to alternative dimensions. Since humans are successful survivors, they presently have no apparent need to migrate. But what if that changes? At the beginning of this book, I said spirituality is not a religion but a destiny. That destiny has nothing to do with faith or belief in a supernatural hereafter. At the core of its being, Life is driven by the need for survival—the primeval spirit. An evolutionary soul could be the answer to its dilemma.

Bibliography

Adams, Fred, *Our Living Multiverse, A Book of Genesis in 0 + 7 Chapters*, Pi Press, 2004

Allman, William F, *Apprentices of Wonder, Inside the Neural Network Revolution*, Bantam, 1989

Armstrong, Karen, *A History of God, From Abraham to the Present: the 4000-year Quest for God*, Vintage, 1993

Asimov, Isaac, *Asimov's New Guide to Science*, Penguin, 1987

Audi, Robert, *The Cambridge Dictionary of Philosophy*, Second Edition, Cambridge, 1999

Baggott, Jim, *A Beginner's Guide to Reality*, Penguin Books, 2005

Banchoff, Thomas F, *Beyond the Third Dimension, Geometry, Computer Graphics, and Higher Dimensions*, Scientific American Library, 1990

Barbieri, Marcello, *The Organic Codes, An Introduction to Semantic Biology*, Cambridge University Press, 2003

Barrett, William, *Death of the Soul, From Descartes to the Computer*, Oxford, 1987

Barrow, John D, *The Constants of Nature, From Alpha to Omega*, Vintage, 2002

Baumann, T Lee, *God at the Speed of Light, The Melding of Science and Spirituality*, Are Press, 2002

Behe, Michael J, *Darwin's Black Box*, Free Press, 2006

Bendit, Lawrence J and Bendit, Phoebe D, *The Etheric Body of Man, The Bridge of Consciousness*, Theosophical Publishing House, 1982

Besant, Annie, Leadbeater, C.W., *Thought-Forms*, The Theosophical Publishing House, 1969

Blackburn, Simon, *Think, A Compelling introduction to Philosophy*, Oxford University Press, 1999

Blackmore, Susan, *The Meme Machine*, Oxford University Press, 1999

Blavatsky, H P, *The Secret Doctrine, The Synthesis of Science, Religion and Philosophy*, The Theosophical Publishing House, 1938

Boslough, John, *Stephen Hawking's Universe*, Fontana, 1984

Brockman, John, *Science at the Edge*, Weidenfeld & Nicolson, 2003

Brockman, John, *The Next Fifty Years, Science in the First Half of the Twenty-First Century*, Weidenfeld & Nicolson, 2002

Brockman, John, *What we Believe but Cannot Prove, Today's Leading Thinkers on Science in the Age of Certainty*, Free Press, 2005

Bruce, Robert, *Astral Dynamics, A New Approach to Out-of-Body Experience*, Hampton Roads, 1999

Buchanon, Mark, *Small World, Uncovering Nature's Hidden Networks*, Phoenix, 2003

Buhlman, William, *Adventures Beyond the Body, How to Experience Out-of-Body Travel*, Harper San Francisco, 1996

Calder, Nigel, *Einstein's Universe, A Guide to the Theory of Relativity*, Penguin, 1990

Calder, Nigel, *Einstein's Universe, The Layperson's Guide*, Penguin, 2005

Callender, Craig and Edney, Ralph, *Introducing Time*, Icon Books, 2002

Cannon, Alexander, *Sleeping Through Space*, The Walcott Publishing Co, 1939

Capra, Fritjof, *The Hidden Connections*, Harper Collins, 2002

Capra, Fritjof, *The Tao of Physics, An Exploration of the Parallels between Modern Physics and Eastern Mysticism*, Flamingo, 1992

Capra, Fritjof, *The Turning Point, Science, Society and the Rising Culture*, Flamingo, 1983

Carter, Rita, *Consciousness*, Weidenfeld & Nicolson, 2002

Casti, John L, *Paradigms Regained, Unravelling the Mysteries of Modern Science*, Abacus, 2000

Cavendish, Richard, *Mythology, An Illustrated Encyclopedia*, Time Warner, 1992

Cayce, Edgar, *Modern Prophet, Four Complete Books*, Gramercy Books, 1990

Chown, Marcus, *The Universe Next Door, Twelve Mind-blowing Ideas from the Cutting Edge of Science*, Review, 2003

Clancy, Paul, Brack, Andre and Horneck, Gerda, *Looking for Life, Searching the Solar System*, Cambridge, 2005

Clegg, Brian, *Light Years, An Exploration of Mankind's Enduring Fascination with Light*, Piatkus, 2001

Collins, *English Dictionary, Third Edition*, Harper Collins, 1991

Collins, Andrew, *Alien Energy, UFO's Ritual Landscapes and the Human Mind*, Eagle Wing Books, 1994

Collins, Andrew, *From the Ashes of Angels, The Forbidden Legacy of a Fallen Race*, Bear & Company, 2001

Cotterell, Arthur, *Encyclopedia of World Mythology*, Parragon, 1999

Coveney, Peter and Highfield, Roger, *The Arrow of Time, The Quest to Solve Science's Greatest Mystery*, Flamingo, 1990

Cremo, Michael A and Thompson, Richard L, *The Hidden History of the Human Race*, Bhaktivedanta, 2002

Darwin, Charles, *The Origin of Species*, Gramercy Books, 1979

Davies, Paul and Gribbin, John, *The Matter Myth, Beyond Chaos and Complexity*, Penguin Books, 1991

Davies, Paul, *About Time, Einstein's Unfinished Revolution*, Penguin Books, 1995

Davies, Paul, *The Edge of Infinity, Beyond the Black Hole*, Penguin, 1994

Davies, Paul, *The Mind of God, Science and the Search for Ultimate Meaning*, Penguin, 1992

Davies, Paul, *The Origin of Life*, Penguin, 2003

Delsemme, Armand, *Our Cosmic Origins, From the Big Bang to the Emergence of Life and Intelligence*, Cambridge, 1998

Devlin, Keith, *The Millennium Problems, The Seven Greatest Unsolved Mathematical Puzzles of Our Time*, Granta Books, 2005

Dunne, J W, *An Experiment with Time*, Faber and Faber, Mcmlviii, 1934

Farthing, Geoffrey A, *Theosophy, What's It All About? Revised Edition*, Theosophical Publishing House, 1983

Ferris, Timothy, *Coming of Age in the Milky Way*, Vintage, 1988

Fisher, Joe, *The Case for Reincarnation*, Grafton Books, 1986

Fisher, Len, *Weighing the Soul, The Evolution of Scientific Beliefs*, Weidenfeld & Nicolson, 2004

Flanagan, Owen, *The Problem of the Soul, Two Visions of Mind and How to Reconcile Them*, Basic Books, 2002

Fontana, David, *Is There An Afterlife?: A Comprehensive Overview of the Evidence*, O Books, 2005

Fraser, Gordon, *The New Physics for the Twenty-First Century*, Cambridge University Press, 2006

Gardner, Laurence, *Bloodline of the Holy Grail, Element Books*, 1996

Geddes & Grosset, *Classical Mythology*, Gresham Publishing, 1995

Gettings, Fred, *Encyclopedia of the Occult, A Guide to Every Aspect of Occult Lore, Belief and Practice*, Rider, 1986

Gleick, James, Chaos, *Making a New Science*, Abacus, 1987

Gleick, James, *Genius, Richard Feynman and Modern Physics*, Abacus, 1992

Gott III, Richard J, *Time Travel in Einstein's Universe, The Physical Possibilities of Travel through Time*, Weidenfeld & Nicolson, 2001

Greene, Brian, *The Elegant Universe, Superstrings, Hidden Dimensions, and the Quest for the Ultimate Theory*, Vintage Books, 1999

Greene, Brian, *The Fabric of the Cosmos, Space, Time, and the Texture of Reality*, Allan Lane, 2004

Gribbin, John and Cherfas, Jeremy, *The First Chimpanzee, In Search of Human Origins*, Penguin, 2001

Gribbin, John, *In Search of Schrödinger's Cat*, Corgi, 1987

Gribbin, John, *In Search of the Big Bang*, Corgi Books, 1992

Gribbin, John, *Schrödinger's Kittens and the Search for Reality*, Weidenfeld & Nicolson, 1995

Gribbin, John, *Science, A History 1543-2001*, Penguin, 2003

Grossinger, Richard, *Embryos, Galaxies and Sentient Beings, How the Universe Makes Life*, North Atlantic Books, 1994

Hamer, Dean H, *The God Gene*, Anchor, 2005

Hancock, Graham, *Flooded Kingdoms of the Ice Age*, Penguin Books, 2003

Hancock, Graham, *Supernatural, Meeting with the Ancient Teachers of Mankind*, Century, 2005

Hawking, Stephen, *A Briefer History of Time*, Bantam Press, 2005

Hawking, Stephen, *The Universe in a Nutshell*, Bantam Press, 2001

Hey, Tony and Walters, Patrick, *The New Quantum Universe*, Cambridge, 2003

Hick, John, *The Fifth Dimension, An Exploration of the Spiritual Realm*, One World, 1999

Horne, Alexander, *Theosophy and the Fourth Dimension*, Theosophical Publishing House, 1928

Hughes-Warrington, Marnie, *Fifty Key Thinkers on History*, Routledge, 2001

Icke, David, *Children of the Matrix*, Bridge of Love, 2001

Icke, David, *The Biggest Secret*, Bridge of Love, 1999

Illingworth, Valerie and Cullerne, J P, *The Penguin Dictionary of Physics*, Penguin, XX

James, Ioan, *Remarkable Physicists, From Galileo to Yukawa*, Cambridge, 2004

Johnson, George, *A Shortcut Through Time, The Path to the Quantum Computer*, Vintage, 2003

Joseph, Frank, *The Destruction of Atlantis, Compelling Evidence of the Sudden Fall of the Legendary Civilization*, Bear & Company, 2004

Kaku, Michio, *Hyperspace, A Scientific Odyssey through Parallel Universes, Time Warps, and the Tenth Dimension*, Oxford, 1994

Kaku, Michio, *Parallel Worlds, The Science of Alternative Universes and our Future in the Cosmos*, Penguin, 2005

King James Version, *The Holy Bible*, American Bible Society, 1981

Klimo, Jon, *Channeling, Investigations on Receiving Information from Paranormal Sources*, North Atlantic Books, 1998

Knight, Christopher and Butler, Alan, *Civilization One, The World is Not as You Thought it Was*, Watkins Publishing, 2004

Koch, Christof, *The Quest for Consciousness, A Neurobiological Approach*, Roberts and Company, 2004

Krauss, Lawrence M, *The Physics of Star Trek*, Harper Collins, 1995

Krauss, Lawrence M, *Hiding in the Mirror, The Mysterious Allure of Extra Dimensions from Plato to String Theory and Beyond*, Viking, 2005

Landsdowne, Zachary F, *The Chakras & Esoteric Healing*, Samuel Weiser, 1986

Lawton, Ian, *Genesis Unveiled, The Lost Wisdom of our Forgotten Ancestors*, Virgin, 2003

Le Poidevin, Robin, *Travels in Four Dimensions, The Enigmas of Space and Time*, Oxford, 2003

Lerner, Eric J, *The Big Bang Never Happened*, Simon & Schuster, 1992

Lewis, Ralph M, *The Conscious Interlude*, Supreme Grand Lodge of Amorc, 1978

Ling, Trevor, *A History of Religion East and West, An Introduction and Interpretation*, MacMillan, 1974

Magueijo, Joao, *Faster than the Speed of Light, The Story of a Scientific Speculation*, William Heinemann, 2003

Marshall, Ian and Zohar, Danah, *Who's Afraid of Schrödinger's Cat?*, Bloomsbury, 1997

Marshall, Reverend Alfred, *The R.S.V Interlinear Greek – English New Testament*, Samuel Bagster and Sons, 1978

Martin, Walter, *The Kingdom of the Cults*, Bethany House, 1985

Mayr, Ernst, *What Evolution Is*, Phoenix, 2001

McCutcheon, Mark, *The Final Theory, Rethinking Our Scientific Legacy*, Universal Publishers, 2004

McDowell, Josh, *Evidence that Demands a Verdict, Historical Evidences for the Christian Faith, Revised Edition*, Christian Art Publishers, 1930

McFadden, Johnjoe, *Quantum Evolution, Life in the Multiverse*, Flamingo, 2000

Microsoft Corporation, *Microsoft Encarta 1993-2005*, 2006

Millar, David, Ian, John and Margaret, *The Cambridge Dictionary of Scientists, Second Edition*, Cambridge, 2002

Narby, Jeremy and Huxley, Francis, *Shamans Through Time*, Thames & Hudson, 2001

Newton, Michael, *Destiny of Souls, New Case Studies of Life Between Lives*, Llewellyn Publications, 2002

Newton, Michael, *Journey of Souls, Case Studies of Life Between Lives*, Llewellyn Publications, 2002

Oerter, Robert, *Mr Tompkins Gets Serious, The Essential George Gamow*, Pi Press, 2006

Oyle, Dr Irving, *Time, Space and the Mind*, Celestial Arts, 1976

Paine, Thomas, *The Age of Reason*, Carol Publishing Group, 1974

Panek, Richard, *The Invisible Century, Einstein, Freud and the Search for Hidden Universes*, Fourth Estate, 2005

Paraphrased, *The Living Bible*, Tyndale House, 1971

Parnia, Dr Sam, *What Happens When We Die, A Ground-Breaking Study into the Nature of Life and Death*, Hay House, 2005

Pearsall, Judy and Trumble, Bill, *Oxford English Reference Dictionary, Second Edition*, Oxford, 2002

Peat, David F, *Superstrings and the Search for the Theory of Everything*, Abacus, 1988

Penrose, Roger, *The Emperor's New Mind, Concerning Computers, Minds and The Laws of Physics*, Vintage, 1990

Powell, Corey S, *God in the Equation, How Einstein Became the Prophet of the New Religious Era*, The Free Press, 2002

Randall, Lisa, *Warped Passages, Unravelling the Mysteries of the Universe's Hidden Dimensions*, Harper Collins, 2005

Rees, Dai and Rose, Steven, *The New Brain Sciences, Perils and Prospects*, Cambridge University Press, 2004

Reichenbach, Hans, *The Philosophy of Space and Time*, Dover, 1957

Revised Standard Version, *The Holy Bible*, Oxford University Press, 1953

Richards, Steve, *The Travellers Guide to the Astral Plane*, The Aquarian Press, 1983

Rohl, David M, *The Lost Testament, From Eden to Exile: The Five-Thousand-Year History of the People of the Bible*, Century, 2002

Rose, Steven, *The 21st Century Brain, Explaining, Mending and Manipulating the Mind*, Jonathan Cape London, 2005

Rucker, Rudy, *The Fourth Dimension*, Penguin, 1986

Rupp, Rebecca, *Four Elements, Water, Air, Fire, Earth*, Profile Books, 2005

Russell, Bertrand, *History of Western Philosophy*, Routledge Classics, 2005

Rutherford, Ward, *Shamanism, The Foundations of Magic*, The Aquarian Press, 1986

Sabom, Michael, *Light and Death, One Doctor's Fascinating Account of Near-Death Experiences*, Zondervan Publishing House, 1998

Schumacher, E.F, *A Guide for the Perplexed*, Abacus, 1977

Scott, Mary, *Kundalini in the Physical World*, Routledge & Kegan Paul, 1983

Scrutton, Robert, *The Message of The Masters*, Jersey Neville Spearman, 1982

Seife, Charles, *Alpha and Omega, The Search for the Beginning and the End of the Universe*, Transworld, 2003

Shanks, Hershel and Witherington III, Ben, *The Brother of Jesus, The Dramatic Story and Meaning of the First Archaeological Link to Jesus and His Family*, Harper, 2003

Sheldrake, Rupert, *The Sense of Being Stared At and Other Aspects of the Extended Mind*, Hutchinson, 2003

Shermer, Michael, *Why People Believe Weird Things*, Henry Holt and Company, 1997

Sitchin, Zecharia, Genesis Revisited, *Is Modern Science Catching Up With Ancient Knowledge?*, Bear & Company, 1991

Sitchin, Zecharia, *When Time Began, Book V of the Earth Chronicles*, Avon Books, 1993

Stafford, Peter, *Psychedelics Encyclopedia, Third Expanded Edition*, Ronin, 1992

Stangroom, Jeremy, *What Scientists Think*, Routledge, 2005

Steiner, Rudolf, *Between Death and Rebirth*, Rudolf Steiner Press, 1975

Steiner, Rudolf, *Occult Science – An Outline*, Rudolf Steiner Press, 1963

Steiner, Rudolf, *The Effects of Spiritual Development*, Rudolf Steiner Press, 1978

Stemman, Roy, *Reincarnation, True Stories of Past Lives*, Piatkus, 1997

Stock, Gregory, *Redesigning Humans, Choosing our Children's Genes*, Profile, 2002

Stokes, Philip, *Philosophy – 100 Essential Thinkers*, Arcturus, 2003

Strong, James, *Strong's Exhaustive Concordance*, Baker Book House, 1983

Susskind, Leonard, *The Cosmic Landscape, String Theory and the Illusion of Intelligent Design*, Little, Brown and Company, 2005

Suzuki, Daisetz Teitaro, *An Introduction to Zen Buddhism*, Rider, 1969

Swedenborg, Emanuel, *Heaven and its Wonders and Hell*, The Swedenborg Society Inc, 1958

Sykes, Brian, *Adam's Curse, A Future Without Men*, Corgi, 2003

Sykes, Brian, *The Seven Daughters of Eve*, Corgi Books, 2002

Talbot, Michael, *The Holographic Universe*, Harper Collins, 1996

Tattersall, Ian, *Becoming Human, Evolution and Human Uniqueness*, Oxford University Press, 1998

Taylor, Timothy, *The Buried Soul, How Humans Invented Death*, Fourth Estate, 2002

Tellinger, Michael, *Slave Species of God*, Music Masters, 2005

Thompson, Mel, *Philosophy of Science*, Hodder & Stoughton Ltd, 2001

Thompson, Ernest, *Spiritualism in the Evolution of Philosophy and Spiritualism in the Evolution of Religion*, Two Worlds Publishing, 1950

Thompson, Thomas L, *The Messiah Myth*, Jonathan Cape, 2005

Von Daniken, Erich, *Chariots of the Gods?*, Souvenir Press, 1993

Von Daniken, Erich, *The Gods and Their Grand Design, The Eighth Wonder of the World*, Corgi Books, 1986

Von Daniken, Erich, *The Gods Were Astronauts, Evidence of the True Identities of the Old 'Gods'*, Vega, 2001

Von Daniken, Erich, *The Return of the Gods, Evidence of Extraterrestrial Visitations*, Element, 1998

Watson, Andrew, *The Quantum Quark*, Cambridge University Press, 2004

Watson, James D and Berry, Andrew, *DNA The Secret of Life*, Arrow Books, 2003

Watson, Lyall, *Supernature II, A New Natural History of the Supernatural*, Sceptre, 1986

Watson, Lyall, *Supernature, A Natural History of the Supernatural*, Sceptre, 1973

Watson, Lyall, *The Romeo Error, A Matter of Life and Death*, Coronet Books, 1974

Watson, Peter, *Ideas, A History From Fire to Freud*, Weidenfeld & Nicolson, 2005

Waugh, Alexander, *Time, From Micro-Seconds to Millennia – A Search for the Right Time*, Headline, 1999

Weinberg, Steven, *Dreams of a Final Theory*, Vintage Books, 1992

Wilber, Ken, *A Theory of Everything, An Integral Vision for Business, Politics, Science and Spirituality*, Gateway, 2000

Williams, Hywell, *Cassell's Chronology of World History, Dates, Events and Ideas that Made History*, Weidenfeld & Nicolson, 2005

Wilmut, Ian, Highfield, Roger, *After Dolly*, Little Brown, 2006

Wright, Robert, *The Moral Animal, Evolutionary Psychology and Everyday Life*, Abacus, 1996

Zimmer, Carl, *Evolution*, Arrow, 2003

Zimmer, Carl, *Soul Made Flesh, The Discovery of the Brain – and How it Changed the World*, Arrow Books, 2004

Zukav, Gary, *The Dancing Wu Li Masters*, Flamingo, 1984

Papers and Articles

Arkani-Hamed, Nima, Dimopoulos, Savas, Dvali, Georgi, *The Universe's Unseen Dimension*s, Scientific American, 2002

Begun, David R, *Planet of the Apes*, Scientific American, August 2005

Bekenstein, Jacob D, *Information in the Holographic Universe*, Scientific American, August 2003

Biello, David, *10th Planet Proves Bigger than Pluto*, Scientific American, 2006

Biello, David, *Supernovae Back Einstein's "Blunder"*, Scientific American, 2005

Biello, David, *Chimp Genome and First Fossils Unveiled*, Scientific American, 2005

Biello, David, Colliding Clusters Shed Light on Dark Matter, Scientific American, 2006

Biello, David, *Neuroscientists Probe Psychedelic Psilocybin*, Scientific American, 2006

Biello, David, *Scientists Predict Extinctions from Global Warming*, Scientific American, 2006

Biello, David, *Separation of Man and Ape Down to Gene Expression,* Scientific American, 2006

Biello, David, *Signs of Early Life in Australian Rocks*, Scientific American, 2006

Blanke, Olaf, Ortigue, Stphanie, Landis, Theodor, Seeck, Margitta, *Neurobiology: Stimulating own-body perceptions,* Nature, September 2002

Bousso, Raphael, Polchinski, Joseph, *The String Theory Landscape*, Scientific American, 2004

Caldwell, Robert R, Kamionkowski, Marc, *Echoes from the Big Bang*, Scientific American, 2002

Caldwell, Robert R, *Quintessence*, Physicsweb, Internet, 2000

Calvin, William H, *The Emergence of Intelligence*, Scientific American, 2006

Cann, Rebecca L, Wilson, Allan C, *The Recent African Genesis of Humans*, Scientific American, 2003

Close, Frank, *To Catch a Rising Star*, New Scientist, 2002

Crick, Francis, Kock Christof, *The Problem of Consciousness*, Scientific American, 2002

Damasio, Antonio R, *How the Brain Creates the Mind*, Scientific American, 2002

Dobbs, David, *Fact or Phrenology*, Scientific American, 2005

Duff, Michael J, *The Theory Formerly Known as Strings*, Scientific American, 2003

Fields, Douglas, R, *Beyond the Neuron Doctrine*, Scientific American, 2006

Ford, Lawrence H, Roman, Thomas A, *Negative Energy, Wormholes and Warp Drive*, Scientific American, 2003

Gazzaniga, Michael S, *The Split Brain Revisited*, Scientific American, 2002

Gould, Stephen J, *The Evolution of Life on Earth*, Scientific American, April 2006

Graham, Sarah, *Chandra Observations Confirm Existence of Dark Energy*, Internet, 2004

Graham, Sarah, *Scorched Remains Suggest Ancient Humans were Firestarters*, Scientific American, 2004

Greene, Brian, *The Future of String Theory*, Scientific American, 2005

Green, J. Timothy, *Near Death Experience, Shamanism, and the Scientific Method*, Internet, IANDS, 1998

Holt, Jim, *Beyond the Standard Model*, Scientific American, 2006

Ingham, Richard, *Chimp DNA Deciphered*, Cool Science, 2005

Ingham, Richard, *'Man of Flores' May Hold the Key to Evolution*, Sapa, 2004

Jogan, Craig J, Kirshner Robert P, Suntzeff Nicholas B, *Surveying Spacetime with Supernovae*, Scientific American, 2002

Kandel, Eric R, *The New Science of Mind*, Scientific American, 2006

Kane, Gordon, *The Dawn of Physics Beyond the Standard Model*, Scientific American, 2005

Kane, Gordon, *The Mysteries of Mass*, Scientific American, 2005

Kearns, Edward, Kajita, Takaaki, Totsuka, Yoji, *Detecting Massive Neutrinos*, Scientific American, 2003

Kokacy, A, *How Does Spending Prolonged Time in Microgravity Affect Astronauts*, Scientific American, 2003

Kole, William J, *Xena Fights for a Place in our Solar System*, Internet, 2006

Kostelecky, Alan, *The Search for Relativity Violations*, Scientific American, 2005

Kraft, Ulrich, *Unleashing Creativity*, Scientific American, 2005

Krauss, Lawrence M, *Cosmological Antigravity*, Scientific American, 2002

Krauss, Lawrence M, Starkman, Glenn D, *The Fate of Life in the Universe*, Scientific American, 2002

Lavine, Marc, *10th Planet Discovered*, Internet, 2005

Lavine, Marc, *US Astronomer Hails 'tenth rock from the sun'*, Internet, 2005

Leonard, William R, *Food for Thought*, Scientific American, 2003

Llewellyn Smith, Chris, *The Large Hadron Collider*, Scientific American, 2003

Logothetis, Nikos K, *Vision: A Window on Consciousness*, Scientific American, 2002

Long, Jeffrey, Bernstein, Paul, *Vision: A Window on Consciousness*, Scientific American, 2002

Lovell, Jeremy, *The Oldest Humans Just Became Older*, Internet, 2005

Luminet, Jean-Pierre, Starkman, Glenn D, Weeks Jefrey R, *Is Space Finite*, Scientific American, 2002

Maldacena, Juan, *The Illusion of Gravity*, Scientific American, 2005

McDonald, Arthur B, Klein, Joshua R, Wark, David L, *Solving the Solar Neutrino Problem*, Scientific American, 2005

Minsky, Marvin, *Will Robots Inherit the Earth?*, Scientific American, October 1994

Nash, Michael R, *The Truth and the Hype of Hypnosis*, Scientific American, 2001

Ostriker, Jeremiah P, Steinhardt, Paul J, *The Quintessential Universe*, Scientific American, 2001

Quinn, Helen R, Witherell, Michael S, *The Asymmetry between Matter*, Scientific American, 2003

Rees, Martin, *Exploring Our Universe and Others*, Scientific American, 2002

Rennie, John, 15 *Answers to Creationist Nonsense*, Scientific American, April 2006

Samsel, W.T, *What is the Law of One?*, Internet, 2000

Sapa, *Amateur Stargazers Stumble Upon New Planet*, Internet, 2005

Schmid, Randolph E, *World's Oldest Jewelry Discovered in South Africa*, Cape Times, 2004

Shapiro, Ehud, Benenson Yaakov, *Bringing DNA Computers to Life*, Scientific American, 2006

Sinclair, David A, Guarente, Lenny, *Unlocking the Secrets of Longevity Genes*, Scientific American, 2006

Starkman, Glenn D, Schwarz, Dominik J, *Is the Universe Out of Tune*, Scientific American, 2005

Tattersall, Ian, *How We Came to Be*, Scientific American, 2006

Tattersall, Ian, *Once we Were Not Alone*, Scientific American, August 2005

Tattersall, Ian, *Out of Africa*, Scientific American, 2003

Tegmark, Max, *Parallel Universes*, Scientific American, May 2003

Thorne, Alan G, Wolpoff, Milford H, *The Multiregional Evolution of Humans*, Scientific American, 2003

Van Lommel, Pim, *About the Continuity of our Consciousness*, Internet, 2005

Van Lommel, Pim, *Medical Evidence for NDE's*, Skeptical Investigations, 2003

Van Lommel, Pim, Van Wees, R, Meyers, V, Elfferich, I, *Near-death experience in survivors of cardiac arrest: a* *prospective study in the Netherlands*, The Lancet, December 2001

Villarreal, Luis P, *Are Viruses Alive?*, Scientific American, 2004

Wayt Gibbs, W, *Ripples in Space Time*, Scientific American, 2002

Weinberg, Steven, *A Unified Physics by 2050?*, Scientific American, 2003

Wolfradt, Uwe, *Strangely Familiar*, Scientific American, 2006

Wong, Kate, *An Ancestor to Call our Own*, Scientific American, January 2003

Wong, Kate, *Chunk of Universes Missing Matter Found*, Scientific American, 2005

Wong, Kate, *Mini Human Species Unearthed*, Scientific American, 2004

Wong, Kate, *The Littlest Human*, Scientific American, February 2005

Wong, Kate, *The Morning of the Modern Mind*, Scientific American, June 2005

Wong, Kate, *Who Were the Neanderthals?*, Scientific American, 2003

Acknowledgments

I owe my gratitude to the members of my family, friends and professionals, who over the decades have helped making this project a success.

I would also like to thank the people who have participated in the creation of the first edition, *Homo Angelicansis*: Robyn Wilkinson for the years of dedication with the layout and contents; Ilse Bigalke for her assistance with proofreading.

Next, I would like to thank Rose Shearer for the countless hours she has invested editing the new edition, *Angelicals Reviewed*.

I would also like to thank *Scribendi* and their team for the professional online editing service they provide. Particularly, I thank EM328 for copyediting the work.

Other titles by Izak Botha

Blood Symbols

Halfway through her Ph.D., Jennifer Jaine's faith has been shaken. She has become convinced that the Catholic church's authority is based on a lie. Desperate to prove herself wrong, she goes to the Vatican, only to be caught up in an international hunt for the truth about the church, the Pope, and how Jesus intended his followers to live their faith.

A stolen artifact, a mysterious murder, and an escaping intruder lead Jennifer from the Vatican to the streets of Rome to the Cave Church of St. Peter in Turkey, where she discovers a secret that could delegitimize the Pope. Chased by scheming cardinals and the trigger-happy head of Vatican security, assisted only by an elderly professor, the son of an Italian Mafioso, and a mysterious—but handsome—Turk, Jennifer must decide whether to become complicit in the church's duplicity or shake the foundations of the planet's most dominant religion.

Semi Finalist—BookLife Prize 2017

About Izak Botha

Izak Botha is a perpetual student of life, a former artist, athlete, performer with the Cape Town City Ballet, counselor, architect, entrepreneur, litigator versus multinational corporations, and now author of *Homo Angelicansis*, *Angelicals Reviewed*, and *Blood Symbols*, which made Semi Finalist in Publishers Weekly's Book Life Prize 2017.

Professor George Claassen of Sceptic South Africa evaluates Botha's writing as "a crucial analysis of evolutionary thinking that deserves to be read with care", while Todd Mercer of Foreword Clarion Reviews applauds for its "inquiry and line of logic that seem beyond the merely plausible—it is urgently imperative."

Settled on South Africa's Garden Route, Botha is presently working on his new novel.

www.ingramcontent.com/pod-product-compliance
Lightning Source LLC
Chambersburg PA
CBHW032111040426
42337CB00040B/184